GENÈVE

The World's Finest Cigars

Flammarion

CONTENTS

Non-Cuban cigars are followed by initials indicating the country of origin
(C: Canary Islands; D: Dominican Republic; H: Honduras; N: Nicaragua).

To my father, who handed down the passion

PREFACE

The idea of representing all the world's greatest cigars is an impossibly gargantuan challenge. In taking up the gauntlet, nevertheless, it is interesting to notice the revolutions, changes, and mutations in the universe of cigars, as well as the eternal truths. While every year—every day—brings innovations, the great classics stand tall; their excellence assures their perennial place of honor.

Since a selection must be made, how do we go about choosing? All of the cigars presented in this book come from our aging rooms. This means they have been conserved under ideal conditions that allow them to live up to their full potential. We used a process of elimination, opting only for those cigars with that special something that sets them apart from the others, however excellent in quality. Finally, the heart has its say. In the final analysis, we are aficionados who have our own personal preferences, leanings, and nostalgia—just like you.

A few comments on our rating system are in order. The term "power" is meant to indicate strength, but also richness of flavor. "Uniformity" is judged in terms of a cigar's fabrication (suppleness, how tightly packed, porosity) and draw, which is essential to the art of smoking. The "character" rating is intended as a point of comparison, not an absolute. All the cigars discussed in these pages are of the highest quality, a term that also bears some defining. A cigar may be impeccable in terms of its tobacco, manufacturing, finish, and maturation, and still not make our final cut. As with any judgement, relativity plays a role. A young vitola can improve greatly in the aging process, an older cigar may have fallen by the wayside and benefit from a reevaluation of its virtues, and time can bring a new verdict on what was long considered an indisputable first choice. Above all, the finest outcomes result from minute differences, subtleties, and nuances that bear noting, to the best of our ability, for the consumer in all of us.

The "Enjoyment" category is designed to provide all the necessary information for optimal smoking pleasure. This includes historical points, affinities with food, wine, alcohol, and circumstances, and suitability with regard to degree of cigar smoking experience. The aim is to sharpen the aficionado's perceptive and analytical skills.

Throughout this book, our one wish is that you finish reading it with your taste buds alerted and your senses awakened, eager to sample one of these, or perhaps some other cigar. This is because we know that a fine cigar demands attention, care, and constant alertness—in other words, passion—to reach its peak. But we also know that the best preparation for savoring a cigar is to dream about it. We hope that this book can be the stuff that dreams are made of.

Vahé Gérard

CUABA SALOMONES

Length: 7¼ in. (184 mm)
Ring Gauge: 57 (22.62 mm)
Body: round
Presentation: traditional box of 10

Look

You open the box like a precious jewel case—before you see what it holds, you are already full of anticipation. Behold a superb massive structure of ten cigars seemingly sculpted from a single block. *Colorado* tones highlight their aristocracy, their perfection in style.

Touch

Firm to the touch, the Cuaba Salomones is also gentle and silky, characterized by an elegance that will enchant lovers of this type of format.

Smell

Complex, the nose is teased by both animal scents—a young and fresh leather—and vegetal ones in the background. The foot, practically closed, is very difficult to distinguish from the overall bouquet.

Taste

Opening with gentle and distant tones, this cigar rapidly swings to a floral world that will accompany the whole of the first third. At the second third, woodsy spices take over, before powerful aromas, rich and unctuous, manifest themselves in the final third, where combustion takes on a greater amplitude. Its architecture marks the passage through each of the aromatic frontiers.

Enjoyment

Originating in the 1950s and then returning to favor at the end of the 1990s, this format allows us to rediscover a product known only to true connoisseurs. It is the ideal companion to sophisticated cuisine, complex wines, and great alcohols that linger on the palate.

OVERALL RATING
Strength: 8 ½ – Uniformity: 9 – Character: 9 ½

SAN CRISTÓBAL DE LA HABANA MURALLAS

Length: 7 ⅛ in. (180 mm)
Ring Gauge: 54 (21.43 mm)
Body: round
Presentation: varnished cabinet of 25

Look

Grace paired with opulence: not only svelte, recalling a churchill in its size, but also powerful, due to a diameter more consequential than that of a double corona, the Murallas (from *muralla* or "wall") demonstrates a superb architecture in very fine, very silky tobacco.

Touch

Its massiveness is impressive: touch alone reveals that this will not be a casual encounter. Never very oily, but silky instead—this is strength and tranquility in one.

Smell

Presented in a bunch, it is rich and perfumed with mellow floral overtones, but these aromas can be misleading, for the taste is in fact very different—except for the first third. Its bouquet in the body proves to be very elegant, with overtones of ripe red berries.

Taste

While the beginning is pure gentleness, mellowness, and woodsy unctuousness, the second third is an outpouring of strong oily aromas evocative of coffee or dark chocolate. The finale provides a powerful explosion that nevertheless stays under control, thanks to the pirámide head leading to warm spices.

Enjoyment

Like the double corona, the rodolfa takes time. The secret lies in a slow and attentive tasting. The Murallas can be marvelously wed with traditional or innovative cuisine, accompanied by a full-bodied red capable of standing up against it.

OVERALL RATING
Strength: 8 ½ – Uniformity: 8 – Character: 8 ½

7

DIPLOMÁTICOS No. 2

Length: 6⅛ in. (156 mm)
Ring Gauge: 52 (20.64 mm)
Body: square
Presentation: traditional box of 25

Look

This rich and full vitola is well-built, with a particularly finely finished head. The *colorado claro* and *maduro* versions both exude strength.

Touch

Flexible rather than soft, this cigar's energetic charge is highlighted by the unctuous mix of humidity and natural fleshiness.

Smell

The rich, long-lasting floral aroma is almost harsh in the first two years, but gains in roundness and nobility as it matures.

Taste

From the first puff, the deep, strong taste might even be overwhelming for a cigar novice. This cigar can be set aside for a few minutes at the sublime mid-point, to enhance the finely concentrated finish, where the humid, spicy aromas turn more woodsy. But the powerful, somewhat hot combustion requires expertise.

Enjoyment

The Diplomáticos No. 2 was formerly eclipsed by the format's brighter stars, but has come into its own in the past decade. It is divine for after-dinner smoking, especially when accompanied by a fine digestive liqueur. Proper aging will soften the initial punch.

OVERALL RATING
Strength: 8 ½ – Uniformity: 8 – Character: 7 ½

H. UPMANN No. 2

Length: 6⅛ in. (156 mm)
Ring Gauge: 52 (20.64 mm)
Body: square
Presentation: traditional box of 25

Look

A cigar with a definite presence, the H. Upmann No. 2's commonly *colorado* wrappers display charismatic red and brown tones. Some more highly veined leaves stand out amid the box's exceptional regularity.

Touch

This is a rigid, compact, homogeneously constructed cigar. Its even foot gives way to a stout body with a perfect pointed copula of a head. Its velvety texture leaves a slight oily film on the skin. Imposing, firm, and masculine.

Smell

The powerful spicy aroma emerges from an amber base to yield the first joys of savoring. The bouquet is marked by highly humid and developed woodsy underbrush notes.

Taste

From the first draw, the flavor is deeply rich and unctuously strong. The H. Upmann No. 2 is exceptionally long in the mouth. The accent is on spicy, peppery, and pungent taste, along the traditional lines of the torpedo format.

Enjoyment

It was years before this great figurado took its rightful place beside the venerable Montecristo No. 2. Contrary to its appearance, the H. Upmann No. 2 is in no way heavy. It is a fine complement to a rich meal for an experienced connoisseur, but not recommended for the novice or occasional smoker.

OVERALL RATING
Strength: 9 – Uniformity: 8 ½ – Character: 9

9

MONTECRISTO No. 2

Length: 6⅛ in. (156 mm)
Ring Gauge: 52 (20.64 mm)
Body: square
Presentation: traditional box of 25

Look

The color range of this king of torpedos runs the gamut of light to dark, with consistent oiliness. The *colorado* is the best-looking of the bunch.

Touch

A perfect body, at once supple and tensed, with a head worthy of a goldsmith. It feels so good in your hand that you'll think you are holding a double corona.

Smell

Immediate and rich, with a spiciness uncharacteristic of the brand. The body exudes a slight leatheriness, while the foot has its own full measure of woodsy, round, rich flavor.

Taste

The first third is more generous than flavorful. Real tastes kick in from there, with striking woodsy, leather, and humid earthy aromas that build into an unguent, spiced finale heightened by the conical tip.

Enjoyment

Often criticized, the Montecristo No. 2 remains a great cigar when properly manufactured. This highly distinctive cigar is in a class of its own and not to be judged by comparison. Perfect after a fine, rich meal along with a unique wine, one that is evocative of sun-drenched climes.

10

OVERALL RATING
Strength: 9 – Uniformity: 8 ½ – Character: 8 ½

PARTAGÁS SÉRIE P No. 2

Length: 6⅛ in. (156 mm)
Ring Gauge: 52 (20.64 mm)
Body: square
Presentation: unvarnished box of 10 or 25

Look

The unctuous coat, typical of the *colorado*, is eye-catching, but it is the ring, identical to that of the famed D4, that really snares attention. This gorgeous cigar, regular in aspect, adopts an air of royalty that inscribes it in the family of legendary models.

Touch

Its unctuous appearance proves to be dry rather than oily. As soon as it is taken in the hand, it exudes a certain power, a charisma that inspires a form of respect before proceeding to the degustation. The body is extremely uniform.

Smell

At first whiff, the Partagás style is recognizable, with an abundance of spices heightened with young leather. The P2 thus offers a rich and memorable bouquet that will be the downfall of many. . . .

Taste

The combustion, more than generous, reveals a slow rise in power, which, at the second third, opens up tastes that are both spicy and unctuous, with a woodiness that is unique among the pirámides. Its remarkable finish, worthy of those of the double coronas, offers an avalanche of aromas.

Enjoyment

The dream cigar to accompany a refined dinner and a heady wine, but preferably at the end of the evening. Be warned, this is a cigar that demands time.

OVERALL RATING
Strength: 7 ½ – Uniformity: 8 ½ – Character: 9

11

SAN CRISTÓBAL DE LA HABANA
LA PUNTA

Length: 6⅛ in. (156 mm)
Ring Gauge: 52 (20.64 mm)
Body: square
Presentation: traditional box of 25

Look

On par with the great torpedos. The San Cristóbal La Punta's silky wrappers range from noble gold to rich red tonalities.

Touch

The uniform construction highlights the leaves' unctuous richness, with a velvety smoothness in the darker colors.

Smell

This cigar is still too young to have come into its own, aroma-wise. The foot's bouquet is green and floral.

Taste

The smooth, aromatic start develops into a powerful, rich second third, with a strong finale. Great performance for such a young vitola, without the overheating common to fledgling cigars.

Enjoyment

The La Punta is a product of the late 1990s, when this type of format was in fashion. It is an excellent addition to an ambitious line with fine unctuousness, staying power, and medium-deep richness. The La Punta is a good choice for dinner with a tannic, woodsy, slightly smoky red wine.

12

OVERALL RATING
Strength: 7 – Uniformity: 8 – Character: 7 ½

VEGAS ROBAINA ÚNICOS

Length: 6⅛ in. (156 mm)
Ring Gauge: 52 (20.64 mm)
Body: square
Presentation: traditional box of 25

Look

This cigar's color is often *claro* or *colorado*; sometimes *maduro*. The handsome gold and brown ring and the veined wrapper leaves make for a distinctive appearance.

Touch

Bulky and packed without over-stuffing, with a delicate smooth surface, good rigidity, and suppleness to boot.

Smell

The foot's subtle green and humid earth nuances yield to rustic, fleshy earth aromas, still with a vegetal note, but never floral.

Taste

This is the new brand's most powerful model. The traditional flavor is apparent from the outset and may be too much for beginners. The rich, heavy taste becomes strong and spicy in the smoking. Roundness and smoothness will improve after a few years' aging.

Enjoyment

For the lover of raw sensations, this generous cigar goes straight to the point of its full flavor. It is ideal after a hearty game dinner, along with a great Armagnac.

13

OVERALL RATING
Strength: 9 – Uniformity: 7 – Character: 6 ½

BOLÍVAR BELICOSOS FINOS

Length: 5 ½ in. (140 mm)
Ring Gauge: 52 (20.64 mm)
Body: round
Presentation: cabinet of 25; traditional box of 25

Look

The cabinet selection displays rhythmically bound packets of chocolaty rods, in hues running the gamut from soft ocher to deep browns, tinged with gold and even green.

Touch

Thick and tender, with a winning suppleness. The perfect ratio between length and girth makes the Belicosos Finos a joy in the hand.

Smell

A full, rich, bouquet of woodsy spices.

Taste

In true torpedo style, the Belicosos Finos starts out smooth, with rich, if fleeting, flavor that develops with stronger, deliciously round, spiced aromas. The conical head lends staying power to the potent finale.

Enjoyment

This torpedo lacks the instantaneous impact and rapid evolution of the robusto model, but makes up for it in complexity, appearance, and bold finish. Good for after-lunch or daytime smoking for spicy-taste lovers. Alcohol does nothing for this cigar. It's a fine vintage on its own.

14

OVERALL RATING
Strength: 7 ½ – Uniformity: 9 – Character: 8

• In the same family, the **Sancho Panza Belicosos** is milder and far more floral.

ROMEO Y JULIETA BELICOSOS

Length: 5½ in. (140 mm)
Ring Gauge: 52 (20.64 mm)
Body: square
Presentation: traditional box of 25

Look

The outstandingly homogeneous, barely veined wrappers make this campana look fit for a king. Deep tones and perfect texture, very oily but not excessively so.

Touch

Elegantly plump, with an elfin head. When not too tightly packed, this cigar is pleasing in the hand: ideally supple and responsive.

Smell

The foot's ample bouquet is distinct from the body's soft leather aroma. Consummately smooth; never cloying.

Taste

From the start, pedigree woodsy spiced flavor, with voluptuous volumes. This is the kind of cigar that leaves you wanting more. When properly made, it burns perfectly, enhanced by the fine torpedo head.

Enjoyment

If only it were a couple of inches longer! This savory cigar leaves you begging for more. Perfect with fish on a fine summer evening, lakeside, with a fruity white wine.

OVERALL RATING
Strength: 7 – Uniformity: 8 – Character: 9

15

SANTA DAMIANA TORPEDO

Length: 6¼ in. (159 mm)
Ring Gauge: 48 (19 mm)
Body: round
Presentation: traditional box of 25

Look
Perfectly symmetrical, with a slightly elongated head that makes for a quicker start. The light golden color is set off by a lovely blue-toned ring.

Touch
Consistent and smooth rather than oily. With a nice heft in the hand. Slightly packed yet supple, especially at the perfectly round foot.

Smell
Primarily vegetal at the foot; honeyed and round in the body. The fragrance is volatile and fleeting, with a lingering freshness uncommon in this format.

Taste
Sweet, smooth start, with a hint of dryness that opens into rich, understated elegance. Flavor builds in the last third to heady, exotic strength.

Enjoyment
This torpedo is a good introduction for newcomers to the format and makes a fine daytime smoke for those in the know. Perfect after a summer dinner; never tiring.

16

OVERALL RATING
Strength: 7 – Uniformity: 7 ½ – Character: 7 ½

• For similar aroma in the same family, try the **Vega Fina Pirámide**.

CUABA EXCLUSIVOS

Length: 5 ¾ in. (145 mm)
Ring Gauge: 45 (17.82 mm)
Body: round
Presentation: traditional box of 25

Look

At a glance, reminiscent of the old-fashioned nineteenth-century Dutch cigar, but the gold inscribed ring, and above all the tobacco, reveal its contemporary spirit.

Touch

Consistent, though tighter at the head than the foot. Firm, with a fine bearing that is not only the effect of its narrowness.

Smell

Fresh and floral, with a dry note. Down to earth. The body brims with slightly acrid hints of fern and green pepper.

Taste

A unique freshness, midway between dry and light, highlights this cigar's woodsy aroma—the most pronounced in the line. The slow start, due to architectonics, builds to the smooth and consistent combustion that makes this model a boon to newcomers.

Enjoyment

A deft mix of sensual elegance, which is hard to pull off, makes the Cuaba Exclusivos a fine addition to this great collection of Cuban cigars.

17

OVERALL RATING

Strength: 6 – Uniformity: 7 – Character: 6 ½

• In the same family, the **Partagás Presidentes** is stronger, longer, and slightly thicker.

HOYO DE MONTERREY PARTICULARES LIMITED EDITION

Length: 9¼ in. (235 mm)
Ring Gauge: 47 (18.65 mm)
Body: round
Presentation: traditional box of 5 in wooden holders

Look

The elegance and beauty of rich, thick maduro tones enhance its imposing length.

Touch

Rich and silky, consistent and resistant. Solidity only minimally compromises suppleness.

Smell

The initially discreet mildness gives way to potent richness, and finishes on a floral, woodsy note.

Taste

True to cigars of these proportions, the Particulares Limited Edition starts off mild, with grassy muted flavor. A sustained woodsy quality dominates the second third, with a hint of non-vegetal spice that deepens in the smoking.

Enjoyment

The prolonged smoking time necessary, largely the result of its compactness, may tire out the novice. However, this cigar is surprisingly manageable for its format. At its best after dinner or with a long winter lunch.

OVERALL RATING

Strength: 8 – Uniformity: 7 – Character: 7

• *In the same family, the* **Sancho Panza Sanchos** *is mellower and lighter in the mouth, with less presence.*

18

MONTECRISTO "A"

Length: 9¼ in. (235 mm)
Ring Gauge: 47 (18.65 mm)
Body: round
Presentation: semi-varnished box of 25

Look

"A" for art in cigar crafting. Whether blond, brown, or dark brown in color, this stunning *especial* sports fine wrappers, masterfully modeled. A jewel in its varnished wood box.

Touch

Silky and smooth, but never soft. Consistent suppleness from foot to head.

Smell

The savory, persistent bouquet penetrates with mellow, lightly woodsy aromas, in a mix of discreet insistence and imposing presence.

Taste

From a nearly imperceptible beginning for this format, the distinct phases are clearly distinguishable. Early vegetal flavor expands to strong woodsy, honeyed leather, and peppery sensations, with a potently spiced yet elegant finale. The transitions are smooth, with silky, melting flavor.

Enjoyment

This mythic model has occasionally suffered in public opinion due to its format. It remains an after-dinner institution to be lingered over. Inexperienced palates tend to be overwhelmed by the Montecristo "A", especially when accompanied with alcohol. The "A" matures beautifully, gaining in roundness and mellowness, and its woodsy note on a Madera backdrop is typical of great vintages.

OVERALL RATING
Strength: 8 – Uniformity: 9 – Character: 9 ½

HOYO DE MONTERREY
DOUBLE CORONAS

Length: 7 ⅝ in. (194 mm)
Ring Gauge: 49 (19.45 mm)
Body: round
Presentation: cabinet of 50; traditional box of 25

Look

Though also available in a box of 25, the cabinet selection, with its 50 bound beauties, is a sight for sore eyes. The uncommonly elegant and uniform gold wrappers encase a silky, unctuous tobacco.

Touch

This generous cigar, with its velvety texture, is like fine silk in the hand. When well preserved, it breathes so beautifully that light pressure gives the illusion of permeability.

Smell

The cabinet selection offers an incomparable unfolding of mild, round, silky gingerbread aromas. Faint at first, the fragrance builds in a rich, persistent intensity of mild spices.

Taste

The heart of this Havana. After an unassuming beginning, a bloom of floral, slightly woodsy taste, never heavy-handed. Roundness and generosity are this venerable model's two pillars of taste.

Enjoyment

With its rare architectural purity of construction, this pedigree grandee is perfect for fish, accompanied by a great white Burgundy.

OVERALL RATING
Strength: 7 – Uniformity: 9 – Character: 9 ½

PARTAGÁS LUSITANIAS

Length: 7 ⅝ in. (194 mm)
Ring Gauge: 49 (19.45 mm)
Body: round
Presentation: cabinet of 50; traditional box of 25

Look

A superb bound bunch running the gilded gamut from light gold to burnished brown. Aesthetic perfection from foot to head.

Touch

Luxurious, velvety wrappers envelope the silky, rich tobacco with high drama. A showstopper body, at once supple and taut.

Smell

A brilliantly nuanced palate of unguent, woodsy potency, marked by generous leather textures. Invigorating in young cigars, rounding with maturity to a broad mellowness, sometimes with a pinch of cinnamon.

Taste

Piercing in the young Lusitanias, with potent woodsy and spiced aromas. The range expands into heavier, more vegetal flavors, without giving up on spiciness. The finale crescendos to a veritable fireworks.

Enjoyment

Unheard of thirty years ago, the Lusitanias is considered a must for this format today. This eclectic cigar goes equally well with a lavish gourmet meal or rustic fare. Best smoked from May to October, with a break in the winter.

OVERALL RATING
Strength: 9 ½ – Uniformity: 9 – Character: 9 ½

21

PUNCH DOUBLE CORONAS

Length: 7⅝ in. (194 mm)
Ring Gauge: 49 (19.45 mm)
Body: round
Presentation: cabinet of 50; traditional box of 25

Look

Breathtakingly gorgeous. This superb rod is state of the art in potency, richness, and pedigree elegance, lending it an exceptional vitality.

Touch

Heavy, compact, strong and yet delicate, with a masculine silkiness, at times a bit oily and charged.

Smell

The scent of a lifetime; one that should never end. The range is rich and complex, with unctuous, woodsy odors on an earthy base. A whole forest of intertwined, meandering olfactory paths.

Taste

The gift of full force from the start. The aromatic register is played out in mild, slightly woodsy flavor that crescendos to a veritable apotheosis that leaves a salty hint on the lips.

Enjoyment

A vitola for the great moments in life, alone or accompanied, but in utter devotion to the cult of smoking. Perfect after an exquisite dinner. This cigar may be a bit much for new smokers. It ages excellently.

OVERALL RATING
Strength: 8 ½ – Uniformity: 8 – Character: 9

• In the same family, the **Saint Luis Rey Prominente** is a marvel of craftsmanship and raw materials, but hard to come by.

RAMÓN ALLONES GIGANTES

Length: 7 ⅝ in. (194 mm)
Ring Gauge: 49 (19.45 mm)
Body: round
Presentation: traditional box of 25

Look

Usually in *maduro* tones, deep and imposing. The red
and gold ring highlights the pleasingly rounded head.

Touch

Supremely silky, rigid and tensed, with a supple bounce
that saves it from excessive hardness.

Smell

Smoked before maturity, the Gigantes wafts hints of new leather and dew-drenched
flowers. The eager, young spices overtake any hint of tobacco aroma. In maturity, this
princely subject scales the heights of voluptuousness, exuding a magical Madera vapor.

Taste

All in the second act. Rich, thick, aromas subtly expand to spicy central tones, to finish
in a symphony of brilliantly condensed bounty.

Enjoyment

One of the least-known double coronas, the Gigantes is an unplundered treasure.
Production is small-scale and reserved for the connoisseurs who swear by it. Perfect to
savor after a fine dinner, with a splendidly aged vintage plum liqueur.

OVERALL RATING
Strength: 9 – Uniformity: 9 – Character: 10

SAINT LUIS REY DOUBLE CORONAS

Length: 7⅝ in. (194 mm)
Ring Gauge: 49 (19.45 mm)
Body: round
Presentation: cabinet of 50

Look

It has the magnificence of a half-wheel in the double corona format, *colorado* in color. From the first glance, it makes its presence felt.

Touch

There was a time when touch was not its strong point, as an inappropriate firmness led to fairly difficult lighting. But the Saint Luis Rey has undergone a makeover, and now marries density with suppleness.

Smell

The nose opens on subtle wet-earth overtones, evolving between fermented grass and dry woodiness. A discreet body, it reveals much more at the foot.

Taste

While the floral debut is faint—as is the case of prominentes—the second phase delivers richer and oilier flavors, but slowly. The finish powerfully deploys blended notes of spices and unctuous cocoa.

Enjoyment

This prominente is not a cigar for everyday consumption, but rather for special moments. It provides a wonderful accompaniment to exotic cuisine or a satisfying ending to a game dinner married with a liqueur.

OVERALL RATING
Strength: 8 ½ – Uniformity: 6 ½ – Character: 7

VEGAS ROBAINA DON ALEJANDRO

Length: 7⅝ in. (194 mm)
Ring Gauge: 49 (19.45 mm)
Body: square
Presentation: traditional box of 25

Look

Sumptuously cloaked, most often in *colorado* tones, and adorned with an elegant brown and gold ring, this double corona is as imposing as it is promising.

Touch

The supple body is so smoothly oiled, that it can leave a fine film on your fingers. The squared shape emphasizes the feeling of uniformity.

Smell

The generous bouquet, greener at the foot and more leathery in the body, foretells strong aroma. The finale is uniquely long-lasting, with a touch of green.

Taste

The harsh flavor when young has been known to turn away some potential admirers. With time, the Don Alejandro gains roundness, and its aggressive taste softens to smooth, deep flavors that retain a satisfying hint of raw freshness. The woodsy aromas become heady and intoxicating with smoking, to finish on mellow, melted tannic notes.

Enjoyment

With its outstanding style and taste, the Don Alejandro is a feather not only in the cap of the Vegas Robaina brand, but of the double corona format in general. Perfect for after dinner, in cool weather, after a continental repast with a fine, hardy Burgundy wine.

OVERALL RATING

Strength: 9 – Uniformity: 9 – Character: 9

25

BOLÍVAR CORONAS GIGANTES CABINET SELECTION

Length: 7 in. (178 mm)
Ring Gauge: 47 (18.65 mm)
Body: round
Presentation: cabinet of 50; traditional box of 25

Look

This cigar's perfect appearance makes it stand out as a great among great churchills. Light or deeper brown in tone, the proud body is topped by an expertly rounded head.

Touch

This seductive heavyweight is robed in smooth and silky, lush wrappers. Supple yet tensed, this cigar should be kept away from dampness, which can soften it. Consistent, personal style.

Smell

The generous bouquet of earth and woodsy scents is never too spicy. This Bolivar's strength exemplifies the brand's tradition. Proper maturation releases its full, resonant force.

Taste

Rich and potent from the second third on, this highly consistent cigar makes each step of its taste evolution apparent to the bona fide smoker. Especially fine after a fish dinner with a heavier white wine.

Enjoyment

26

Long unavailable to the general public, this discreet cigar wins for its consistency. It makes a fine vintage. The cabinet selection of 50 is preferable to the traditional box for its superior bouquet.

OVERALL RATING
Strength: 8 – Uniformity: 7 ½ – Character: 8 ½

• In the same family, the **Sancho Panza Coronas Gigantes** is more earthy and milder.

COHIBA ESPLÉNDIDOS

Length: 7 in. (178 mm)
Ring Gauge: 47 (18.65 mm)
Body: round
Presentation: varnished presentation box of 25;
case of 3

Look

The varnished box offers this cigar the most sumptuous presentation imaginable for a churchill. Most often clad in *colorado* or *claro*, this cigar has a fine and regular cap that catches the eye as soon as the box is opened.

Touch

With a gorgeous roundness that increases the pleasantness of tactile sensations, this aristocrat proves to be silky without being overly oily or sticky. All the same, the density of tobacco can give it a certain hardness. We prefer more unctuous varieties.

Smell

Overtones of young fresh leather, heightened with a touch of spice, more floral and riper in bouquet, it can give an initial impression of discretion. But this is only a fleeting impression.

Taste

This rich-tasting churchill exudes, from the outset, peppery aromas heightened with tannins that persist until the end of the second third—the final third can go as far as being piquant.

Enjoyment

The Espléndidos prides itself on being a great post-dinner cigar, a welcome accompaniment for fine wines. Its power allows it to prolong pleasure. After a rough patch when rivals arrived on the scene, it serenely regained its spot among the top twenty. But attention needs to be paid so that it does not weaken in consistency.

OVERALL RATING
Strength: 9 – Uniformity: 6 ½ – Character: 7

27

LA GLORIA CUBANA TAÍNOS

Length: 7 in. (178 mm)
Ring Gauge: 47 (18.65 mm)
Body: round
Presentation: traditional box of 10

Look

Open the box and the ten cigars are a pure work of art, ringed in gold and wrapped in deep, rich brown. The aromatic hints are borne out in the smoking.

Touch

Thick, supple, and taut. The Taínos can sometimes be a bit tightly wound at the head, but the body is consistently uniform. Fragile at the foot like all fine larger models, it is nonetheless well built, solid, and imposing.

Smell

The discreet, subtle aroma of well-oiled leather. The spicy notes, concentrated at the foot, bring out the woodsy, ambered character of the classic scent.

Taste

Rich and potent, the Taínos' flavor range is deep, round, and expansive, delivering sustained, substantial woodsy and spiced flavors in the mouth. The overall impression is exceptionally harmonious for this format.

Enjoyment

This truly grand cigar is especially fine when aged. Its one fault is synonymous with its greatest attribute: its uncommonness. For cigar connoisseurs, its complexity and consistency make a rare after-dinner treat. Unforgettable in the company of a fine, tannic Bordeaux wine.

28

OVERALL RATING
Strength: 8 ½ – Uniformity: 8 – Character: 8 ½

• In the same family, the **Partagás Churchills de Luxe** is less elegant in appearance and spicier in flavor.

H. UPMANN SIR WINSTON

Length: 7 in. (178 mm)
Ring Gauge: 47 (18.65 mm)
Body: round
Presentation: semi-varnished box of 25

Look

The old, deep green box brought to mind a cask of precious emeralds. The new varnished wood casing is equally elegant. These majestic churchills range from pale honey to black chocolate in color. The range includes a sumptuous, uniquely intense *maduro* hue.

Touch

Crafted with only the finest wrapper leaves, the Sir Winston is both rugged and smooth to the touch, with an underlying silkiness.

Smell

Particularly woodsy and green at its youngest, the Sir Winston gains depth and thickness with age. The central note of dark cacao is highly developed, round, and imposing.

Taste

Impeccably potent and elegant, this great churchill generously deploys its spicy, strong aroma. Amber hints incise the flavor on your palate. This cigar is indisputably for true connoisseurs of the format.

Enjoyment

Made for great occasions, this indefatigable depth player will completely win you over. The occasional, slight imperfections are outweighed by the outstanding overall quality.

OVERALL RATING

Strength: 9 – Uniformity: 7 ½ – Character: 8 ½

• In the same family, the **Cohiba Esplendidos** allies class with panache.

29

PUNCH CHURCHILLS

Length: 7 in. (178 mm)
Ring Gauge: 47 (18.65 mm)
Body: round
Presentation: cabinet of 50; traditional box of 25

Look

Less elegant but more ample than the Punch double corona, the Punch Churchills is a pedigree breed. The half wheel shows off a round of perfectly modeled heads. The color range tends towards dark brown, with an occasional, dazzling *claro*.

Touch

As usual for the Punch brand, unctuous richness and velvety texture win out over silkiness. More taut than pliable, the body is not short on suppleness.

Smell

At first highly vegetal, the aroma quickly develops in earthy tonalities of wet hay and rain-ploughed fields; scents that will move you inside. The body exudes the warmth of humid leather, underlined by a powdery dash of spice.

Taste

The young Punch Churchills is earthy, tannic, and thick, never dry or flat. With age, the flavor develops a fine woodsy range, heady and peppery. The vintage cigar's roundness perfectly melds all the registers.

Enjoyment

This cigar's richness makes it a rewarding after-dinner treat. Excellent with a fine rum: earthiness complementing its woodsy flavor.

OVERALL RATING

Strength: 9 ½ – Uniformity: 8 – Character: 9

• In the same family, the **Romeo y Julieta Prince of Wales** *is slightly less earthy, and more vegetal.*

30

EL REY DEL MUNDO TAÍNOS

Length: 7 in. (178 mm)
Ring Gauge: 47 (18.65 mm)
Body: round
Presentation: unvarnished box of 25

Look

This handsome churchill's fine, silky wrappers range from pale to deep in color. Though lovers of the brand show a preference for the *claro* tone, the *maduro claro* happens to suit it to a T.

Touch

Supple and firm at the same time, with a highly regular consistency. This cigar is smooth to the touch and feels just right in the hand.

Smell

The scent starts off subtly, then unfolds through woodsy, almost dry tonalities to expand into the light, fresh, round aromas of new leather.

Taste

This well-engineered churchill opens out in a mild, slow aromatic journey. The start is on the woodsy side, while the middle's poised, heavy tonalities rank this cigar among the grandees.

Enjoyment

With its reputation as the lightest of Cuban julietas, the El Rey del Mundo Taínos is often overshadowed by the format's star models. It deserves a place of honor among this fine family, and is ideal after lunch in the country or with champagne. The woodsy flavor is a great taste compliment to the freshness of an extra-brut champagne.

OVERALL RATING

Strength: 5 – Uniformity: 7 – Character: 7

• In the same family, the **Hoyo de Monterrey Churchills** is more consistent, yet mild.

31

ROMEO Y JULIETA CHURCHILLS

Length: 7 in. (178 mm)
Ring Gauge: 47 (18.65 mm)
Body: square
Presentation: traditional box of 25,
with or without aluminum tubes

Look

The traditional squared presentation (without the tube) comes in a wide range of hues, with deep *maduro* predominating. Good regularity, despite the veiny wrappers.

Touch

Inconsistent manufacturing runs the gamut from flaccid mushiness to over-packed. Ideally between the two extremes, this churchill is supple rather than soft, with finely oiled wrappers. The head is round and the body straight and erect, making it a pleasure in the hand.

Smell

After a highly floral outset, bolder, more horsy aromas of stables and leather take the lead. A greenish background note heralds a substantial cigar.

Taste

Despite the lamentably irregular quality, at its best, this mythic vitola deploys a fine, spiced aromatic palate. It is rustic and not round, but rich and strong into the last third. Though its finale is full force, the Romeo y Julieta Churchills burns balanced, easy, and consistent.

Enjoyment

Perfect after a winter dinner, with an old Armagnac that adds to its great dimensionality.

OVERALL RATING

Strength: 9 – Uniformity: 6 – Character: 6 ½

SAINT LUIS REY CHURCHILLS

Length: 7 in. (178 mm)
Ring Gauge: 47 (18.65 mm)
Body: round
Presentation: cabinet of 50; traditional box of 25

Look

In golden tones, never darker than *colorado*, this stylish cigar is a wonder of architectural consistency.

Touch

Supple and velvety, more silky than oily, slightly rough, this cigar is perfectly consistent and homogeneous from foot to head. Well-balanced, highly satisfying in the hand.

Smell

The full bouquet comes quickly to the fore, accented with woodsy, slightly spicy aromas on an unguent cacao backdrop. Essentially round, bold, and richly earthy. Precision interwoven with nobility.

Taste

Superior combustion deploys the unctuous aromas that become strong by the end of the first third. The tone is exotic and spicy, with a touch of dryness.

Enjoyment

Also available in a box of 25, the cabinet selection of 50 allows this fine blend to mature to perfection, releasing supremely refined honeyed and woodsy flavor. This churchill is ideal for slow savoring after a fine French, Italian, or Asian meal.

OVERALL RATING

Strength: 8 – Uniformity: 8 – Character: 9

• *In the same family, the **H. Upmann Monarcas** (with or without tubes) is well constructed and more earthy in flavor.*

33

SAN CRISTÓBAL DE LA HABANA EL MORRO

Length: 7 in. (178 mm)
Ring Gauge: 47 (18.65 mm)
Body: square
Presentation: traditional box of 25

Look

With their resplendent *colorado* hues, these cigars are as tempting as the milk chocolate they bring to mind.

Touch

The El Morro is rich, thick, and noble to the touch, with a slight tendency to fullness.
A generously proportioned cigar.

Smell

This full-bodied cigar hides behind an initially modest façade. Slightly spiced earthy tones develop into a core of moist underbrush. The completely moist aroma range explains the slow start.

Taste

The foot is a bit distant and light, while the second third is full and round, stopping just short of heavy. The ripe, earthy, slightly peppery flavor opens into a powerful finale.

Enjoyment

This recent brand, founded in 1999, has yet to win unanimous approval. A new line is always worth discovering, especially one that has variety on its side. The El Morro should take its place among lovers of rich, complex flavor, once its full potential is brought out with maturation. The vitolas are designed to accompany a great, full-blown Burgundy after a down-home meal.

OVERALL RATING
Strength: 7 – Uniformity: 8 – Character: 8 ½

MONTECRISTO CORONAS GRANDES

Length: 5 ¾ in. (146 mm)
Ring Gauge: 48 (19 mm)
Body: round
Presentation: traditional box of 25,
individually cellophane wrapped

Look

This handsome cigar is wrapped in hues from golden yellow to light brown. The dark brown ring distinguishes it from Cuban Montecristos. The body's perfect roundness is prolonged in the head, making for an elegant whole.

Touch

At once supple and taut, this highly regular cigar is a joy in the hand.

Smell

Vegetal and woodsy at the foot, with a moist leather scent in the body. The short-lived aromas are delivered by a whiff of green characteristic of this type of blend.

Taste

An astonishing freshness, followed by a wonderful smoothness. The thick notes are almost absent, replaced by nicely rounded woody aroma. But beware, an overly quick draw could lead to unpleasant overheating.

Enjoyment

Perfect for newcomers to this format, the Coronas Grandes is fine for a before dinner drink, and will not ruin the taste buds or appetite for eating. The combustion is rhythmic and slow. This cigar is available only in the United States and the Dominican Republic.

OVERALL RATING
Strength: 6 ½ – Uniformity: 9 – Character: 8 ½

35

COHIBA SIGLO VI

Length: 5 ⅞ in. (150 mm)
Ring Gauge: 52 (20.64 mm)
Body: round
Presentation: varnished cabinet of 10 or 25;
case of 3, with protection tubes

Look

As is its custom, Cohiba has mastered an immaculate presentation: as soon as the bunch of cigars emerges from its presentation box, we are impressed by the beauty of its volume and the finesse of its composition.
Often silky rather than oily, it acquires a certain luster that is highly becoming.

Touch

The size-to-diameter harmony is immediately attractive. Its firm structure is well balanced by a slight moistness. A cigar to begin savoring as soon as it is between your fingers.

Smell

Rich in exotic savors, the bouquet of the Siglo VI remains opulent and strong in animal scent, in an ensemble of mellow headiness.

Taste

The beginning is not aggressive. It is in the last two-thirds that rich and unctuous fragrances develop, more woodsy than animal. The vegetal aspect gradually gives way to very distinctive aromas of tanned leather.

Enjoyment

Superbly manufactured, the Siglo VI always proves to be extremely generous and burns very evenly. An evening cigar, it is a fitting accompaniment for a fine dinner and the great reds of the Rhône Valley—and the two hours that follow. Only for confirmed lovers.

OVERALL RATING
Strength: 7 ½ – Uniformity: 9 – Character: 9 ½

TRINIDAD ROBUSTOS EXTRA

Length: 6⅛ in. (155 mm)
Ring Gauge: 50 (19.84 mm)
Body: round
Presentation: varnished box of 12; case of 3

Look

Silky and soft in appearance, this cigar is a marvel of craftsmanship, with a perfectly balanced size-to-diameter proportion. Most often composed of golden tobacco, it offers itself to the eyes as a genuine little gem of Cuban art.

Touch

A pleasure to handle, both moist and firm, it seizes attention with its extremely fine texture—a fragility that creates the beauty of the grain.

Smell

The blend, very woodsy and fresh, remains discreet: appreciation, here, is not a matter of diving into a mass, but rather savoring the elegance of the bouquet from the surface.

Taste

Truly representative of the start of the 2000s, the Robustos Extra is very aromatic, with sweet woodsy overtones. The second third is strong, with more unctuous and floral notes, before a more sustained final third, which, without becoming spicy, presents an extraordinary fluidity.

Enjoyment

Over the years, the Robustos Extra has—thanks to its perfect balance—built up a family of followers. Often consumed after lunch or dinner, it also offers the occasional lover the pleasure of an easy degustation. Highly recommended for summer meals, there is no better companion for moments of relaxation at the waterside.

37

OVERALL RATING

Strength: 5 ½ – Uniformity: 8 ½ – Character: 9

COHIBA SIGLO IV

Length: 5 ⅝ in. (143 mm)
Ring Gauge: 46 (18.26 mm)
Body: round
Presentation: traditional box of 25

Look

The mass is generous and the construction majestic. Most often ranging gold to deep *maduro* in color, with a few *claro* or bright *colorado* exceptions, the Siglo IV has the silky elegance of a great, exceptionally balanced gran corona.

Touch

This velvety, lush cigar feels good in the hand. Grasped too tightly, it becomes difficult to draw smoke.

Smell

Overflowing with spicy and woody scents at the head, the aroma is much more vegetal at the foot, but the intensity continues.

Taste

The Siglo IV's richness and strength is typical of the Cohiba brand. Its potent, unctuous, round spice flavors remain into the last third, with exceptional generosity. Long in the mouth and well oiled, this cigar leaves a lasting impression on the palate.

Enjoyment

The competition is heavy among corona gorda, but the Siglo IV is definitely at the top of the heap. It has the advantage of uniqueness, and stands out among the others. Perfect after dinner with a fine Armagnac, this cigar is for experienced smokers who can appreciate the concentrated strength of its last third. It makes a fine vintage.

OVERALL RATING

Strength: 8 – Uniformity: 8 ½ – Character: 9

• *In the same family, the **Bolívar Coronas Extra** is less refined, yet strong.*

38

HOYO DE MONTERREY ÉPICURE No. 1

Length: 5 ⅝ in. (143 mm)
Ring Gauge: 46 (18.26 mm)
Body: round
Presentation: cabinet of 50 or 25

Look

Though available in a 25-piece cabinet version, the half wheel presentation is stunning. The bundle's beauty speaks for itself, its tones ranging from gold to *maduro*, with a few light green variants along the way.

Touch

Perfect balance between diameter and size emphasizes the silky roundness, very fine to the touch. A grand model with imposing presence.

Smell

The Épicure No. 1 is highly scented, in a consistent floral, thick range sometimes accented with the dry, greenish hint characteristic of floral cigars. The second wave is deeper, with rich cacao tonalities.

Taste

In keeping with the brand's venerable tradition, the first, highly vegetal puffs softly fade. It is only well into the second third that the developed, unctuous richness begins to meld with the woodsy aromas. The final third is slightly more concentrated.

Enjoyment

Like the No. 2 (robusto), which has long been in favor, the Épicure No. 1 deserves top billing. Perfect after a light summer meal with a fruity white wine or a less tannic red, the cigar is also fine after lunch and will not tire the smoker out.

39

OVERALL RATING

Strength: 6 – Uniformity: 9 – Character: 8 ½

• *In the same family, the **Punch-Punch de Luxe** is similarly light, but more grassy and earthy.*

H. UPMANN MAGNUM 46

Length: 5⅝ in. (143 mm)
Ring Gauge: 46 (18.26 mm)
Body: round
Presentation: cabinet of 25

Look

A bundle of gran coronas in all its possible glory. Outstandingly crafted, with a rich chromatic range running from *claro* to *colorado*.

Touch

Packed yet highly supple, the Magnum 46 is a heavyweight, as you can tell from lifting the bundle. Particularly unctuous and silky without being velvety, this cigar sometimes leaves a trace of oil behind on the waxed paper.

Smell

This noble beast exudes woodsy, delicately spiced scents, opening to a cacao core with deep notes of lightly tanned leather. The bouquet is irresistibly tempting.

Taste

After a slow start, the taste quickly builds to woodsy spices with an exotic accent. The finale is thick and round, almost heady. An atypical H. Upmann.

Enjoyment

This cigar's beauty is due above all to its superior homogeneity and consistency; no small order for such small-scale production. Its limited availability is also part of its appeal among a handful of aficionados. Among corona gorda specialists the Magnum 46 is prized for its aromatic range. Ideal after dining on fish or fowl.

OVERALL RATING

Strength: 7 – Uniformity: 9 – Character: 9 ½

• In the same family, the **H. Upmann Super Coronas**, which is produced in a limited edition, is high in regularity and quality.

JUAN LÓPEZ SELECCIÓN No. 1

Length: 5 ⅝ in. (143 mm)
Ring Gauge: 46 (18.26 mm)
Body: round
Presentation: cabinet of 25

Look

A bound bunch of Juan López No. 1 exudes purity and integrity. The unringed wrappers are generally *claro* or *colorado claro*; occasionally *maduro* in hue. The round heads are exceptionally consistent.

Touch

More silky than oily in the hand, with a robust feel of suppleness and perfect porosity. The round head and foot are slightly firm without being compact. The no-nonsense texture is to the touch what the straightforward scent is to the smell.

Smell

Starting from the foot, the scents are direct, rich, round, and cacao-tinged. They develop in woodsy dimensionality on a leather backdrop for true aromatic fireworks.

Taste

Generous flavor from the start, with a mix of vegetal and earthy tastes. The last third releases woodsy flavors with a touch of moist spice.

Enjoyment

Indisputably among the crown jewels of the corona gorda, this superior cigar has the added plus of never tiring a smoker, thanks to a wonderfully effortless combustion, exceptional for the format. Perfect for exotic cuisine.

OVERALL RATING

Strength: 7 ½ – Uniformity: 8 ½ – Character: 9

41

PUNCH ROYAL SELECTION No. 11

Length: 5 ⅝ in. (143 mm)
Ring Gauge: 46 (18.26 mm)
Body: round
Presentation: cabinet of 25

Look

The bundle presentation complements the fine construction of this young, elegant cigar. Colors range from very pale *claro* to a rich dark brown, by way of light green hues.

Touch

Supple and dense at the same time, this gran corona's wrapper is smooth to the touch. With its outstanding balance and perfect roundness, it feels good in the hand.

Smell

The highly floral, slightly thick bouquet is atypical for the Punch brand. The scent is intensified with a ripe vegetal tonality accented by an earthy hint.

Taste

The flavor sensation opens in an aromatic floral key: round, honeyed, congenial, and uncomplicated by spices. This expands in a highly original way to take on fresh earthy notes that balance the overall richness.

Enjoyment

This undeniably great Havana's flavorful complexity echoes its architectural simplicity. Inveterate admirers are thrilled to have it back in circulation after a long time off the market. Savor this great cigar after a meal of grilled sea bass with a fruity white wine, on a fine summer's eve, outdoors. Unforgettable.

OVERALL RATING
Strength: 7 – Uniformity: 9 – Character: 9 ½

PUNCH PUNCH-PUNCH

Length: 5 ⅝ in. (143 mm)
Ring Gauge: 46 (18.26 mm)
Body: sets of 25 square or 50 round
Presentation: traditional box of 25; cabinet of 50

Look

The ultimate classic: with caps ranging from *claro* to *colorado*, it seduces a wide public as its corona gorda format reassures lovers little inclined to take on large ring gauges.

Touch

It is above all the moistness that makes an impression (at least when it is not rolled too tightly). Pleasant to handle, it is extremely elegant, with an unctuous, sometimes slightly granulated character due to skin a little on the thick side.

Smell

The Punch-Punch is the most floral of this great family known for its richness and earthiness. Almost too discreet, it could well be confused with the identically sized Épicure No. 1 from Hoyo de Monterrey in a blindfold test. It is distinctive for a certain olfactory freshness, reminiscent of the countryside at the birth of spring.

Taste

Its fresh and vegetal first third sets the tempo: the ripe fruit aromas to follow never become strong or powerful. Therein lies all its charm, with this touch of unctuousness that confers upon it a certain roundness.

Enjoyment

While this fine cigar may be no novelty, it has only gained prominence in the last twenty-five years, as it deepens in aromatic subtlety and mellowness. It thus aligns classicism and originality in taste.

OVERALL RATING
Strength: 6 – Uniformity: 8 – Character: 9

RAFAEL GONZÁLEZ
CORONAS EXTRA

Length: 5⅝ in. (143 mm)
Ring Gauge: 46 (18.26 mm)
Body: square
Presentation: traditional box of 25

Look

This supremely uniform, pedigree cigar struts its stuff in
claro to *colorado* wrappers. Never quite oily, it exudes a
silky, consistent, slightly austere elegance.

Touch

Rigor and rectitude from foot to head are the Coronas Extra's motto. Perfection through
and through, in suppleness and density alike.

Smell

The highly aromatic scent recalls the Montecristos of the 1960s. Rich tonalities lend
intensity to the woodsy core sheathed in floral notes. Enchanting.

Taste

The consistent, generous flavor builds in richness as it burns. Freshness expands with
round, ample woodsy notes. This cigar never overheats or attacks the palate, but remains
gentlemanly from start to finish.

Enjoyment

Although favored by many lovers of traditional Havanas, the Rafael González deserves an
even greater measure of renown. Its small scale production may in part be the
reason for its limited recognition. This cigar is excellent for after dinner or receptions,
where its accessible side should bring it to the attention of a larger public.

44

OVERALL RATING

Strength: 7 – Uniformity: 8 – Character: 9

EL REY DEL MUNDO
GRAN CORONAS

Length: 5⅝ in. (143 mm)
Ring Gauge: 46 (18.26 mm)
Body: square
Presentation: semi-varnished box of 25

Look

Generally more *maduro* than other models of the brand, the Gran Coronas is uniform in appearance, quite similar to what is created by Punch or Rafael González. Less unctuous, it is however no less a stunning object.

Touch

Slightly dry and supple, its square body fills out over time. Easy to the touch, it offers a good size-to-diameter balance. The only weak point: the thinness of its cap.

Smell

Delicately floral and dusky, it gives off a faint and linear scent, only delivering charming notes of toasted hazelnuts once it has been lit.

Taste

Light and agreeable. While a muted start gives it a slightly dry aspect in the mouth, it gradually opens up to more woodsy aromas, but always discreetly. The finish is more unctuous without being overly so, thus allowing for easy digestion. It can make an excellent vintage, with a slightly maderized aspect that is highly attractive.

Enjoyment

Although this brand remains in the shadow of the greats, its corona gorda is an excellent daytime cigar, an ideal accompaniment for moments of relaxation as well as for working hours. True, it is not a pearl of refined degustation, but it will initiate beginners to the joys of the after-lunch cigar.

45

OVERALL RATING

Strength: 5 – Uniformity: 7 – Character: 8

SAINT LUIS REY SÉRIE A

Length: 5 ⅝ in. (143 mm)
Ring Gauge: 46 (18.26 mm)
Body: round
Presentation: cabinet of 50, traditional box of 25

Look

The half wheel is perfect from foot to head, with exemplary roundness. The color range goes from *claro* to deep *maduro*, by way of green tones.

Touch

The lightly velvety wrapper binds a stunningly packed body. The fact that this special quality is only to be found in the cabinet selection, not in the box of 25, shows just how difficult it is to control the quality of a hand-crafted product.

Smell

The initial, seductive cacao scent opens into more floral vistas which, in the younger cigars, tends to fermented fragrance. The body exhales woodsy, dry aromas with a greenish character.

Taste

Rich, round and hardy, without excessive strength, this cigar is a feat of artistic flavoring. The start is on the light side, with a rounder, richer middle third marked by aromatic spices. The finale is full and generous.

Enjoyment

46

This handsome corona gorda fits well with today's preference for plenty of taste and presence without aggressivity. With its superior lasting power in the mouth, it makes a fine after-lunch or after-dinner smoke.

OVERALL RATING
Strength: 7 ½ – Uniformity: 8 – Character: 8 ½

SAN CRISTÓBAL DE LA HABANA
LA FUERZA

Length: 5⅝ in. (143 mm)
Ring Gauge: 46 (18.26 mm)
Body: square
Presentation: traditional box of 25

Look

This majestic gran corona resembles a double corona, minus the last third. Stouter than most of its brothers, it generally sports *colorado* coloring, never *maduro*.

Touch

Firm, thick, and at times just a hair short of too tightly packed, this cigar is no easy or quick smoke, despite its extra girth. The uniform construction, silky feel, and generous proportions make for a pleasing heft in the hand.

Smell

Like the El Morro, the La Fuerza's first third is understated. It is not until you are into the second third that seductively round, woodsy aromas take over. Not to be confused with a churchill.

Taste

Highly satisfying when not overly packed, this cigar is initially herbaceous and fresh. It builds in subtlety, with classic woodsy, unctuous notes. The rich, tasty finale's fine longness will make you forgive the slow start.

Enjoyment

This talented new arrival should be given the benefit of time before passing judgement. It will be fascinating to compare the young cigars with their mature counterparts in a few years' time.

OVERALL RATING

Strength: 7 – Uniformity: 8 ½ – Character: 9

47

MONTECRISTO EDMUNDOS

Length: 5 ¼ in. (135 mm)
Ring Gauge: 52 (20.64 mm)
Body: round
Presentation: unvarnished box of 25; case of 3,
with protection tubes

Look

A beautiful presentation box houses rounded and truly appetizing cigars, extremely uniform, ranging from *clarissimo* to *colorado-claro*.

Touch

Sometimes more moist than supple as a result of its fleshy body, the Edmundos fills the hand and has a real presence. Generally silky and smooth, it is seductive to the touch.

Smell

Fresh and agreeable, the nose is met with a green tea fragrance that reassures us, beckoning us to taste it.

Taste

A break from the traditional line of this great brand, the Edmundos is the incarnation of a new style at Montecristo: its vegetal and woodsy nuances set an aromatic tempo that is very accessible in the first third, before becoming richer and evolving towards young leather.

Enjoyment

A great cigar in the kingdom of robustos. Here, Montecristo has drawn nearer to aromas and flavors cherished by a whole generation of cigar lovers who have found the Edmundos to be an excellent "multifunctional" cigar, a joyful companion for all moments of the day.

OVERALL RATING
Strength: 5 – Uniformity: 7 ½ – Character: 9 ½

H. UPMANN CONNOISSEUR No. 1

Length: 5 in. (127 mm)
Ring Gauge: 48 (19.05 mm)
Body: round
Presentation: cabinet of 25

Look

The 25-piece bundle tends to *colorado claro* tones. This finely engineered robusto is exceedingly uniform, challenging the Hoyo de Monterrey Épicure No. 2 for top honors in its category.

Touch

The smooth, somewhat silky wrappers house a tensed, supple body, loosely packed to the point of feebleness at times. A jewel of fine crafting.

Smell

A spring bouquet, highly floral and never heady. The generously oiled core brings beef broth to mind, at times with a touch of young, bracing leather. Fully present but never heavy or intoxicating, the scent is pure pleasantness.

Taste

Always light, never dull, the Connoisseur No. 1 deploys a rich, unctuous aromatic range of exotically tweaked, woodsy flavor. The fresh start opens into a more fruity end. The overall fine construction never bogs down with time.

Enjoyment

This accessible, easy, companionable cigar has remained in the shadows far too long. It can be smoked at any time of day. Good maturation is sufficient; extensive aging does nothing to improve it.

OVERALL RATING

Strength: 6 – Uniformity: 9 – Character: 8 ½

• In the same family, the **Hoyo de Monterrey Épicure No. 2** is an arch rival, and perfectly complementary.

EL REY DEL MUNDO
CABINET SELECCIÓN CHOIX SUPRÊME

Length: 5 in. (127 mm)
Ring Gauge: 48 (19.05 mm)
Body: round
Presentation: cabinet of 50, traditional box of 25

Look

This pale-colored robusto, nearly matte blond in tone, is similar to the Romeo y Julieta Exhibición No. 4 and the Saint Luis Rey Regios.

Touch

At once silky and smooth, this cigar is the only one in its format to offer a perfect combination of consistency, suppleness, and flexibility.

Smell

The floral bouquet, with no spicy or harsh overtones, exudes a mild freshness uncommon in cigars.

Taste

The generous combustion deploys fresh, creamy notes accented with a salty taste on the lips. The smoothly uniform aromatic unfolding is never tiring. There is no doubt that this is a cigar with winning ways.

Enjoyment

The Choix Suprême has been around for more than forty years. After taking its time to make itself known, it is now recognized as an excellent smoke for a beginning Epicurean. Experienced aficionados enjoy the Choix Suprême in the morning, after lunch, or as a second evening cigar, when the taste buds start to tire.
This cigar is more complexly flavorful in the cabinet selection than in the 25-piece box. No long maturation is needed.

50

OVERALL RATING
Strength: 6 – Uniformity: 8 – Character: 8 ½

ROMEO Y JULIETA EXHIBICIÓN No. 4 CABINET SELECCIÓN

Length: 5 in. (127 mm)
Ring Gauge: 48 (19.05 mm)
Body: round
Presentation: cabinet of 50, traditional box of 25

Look

This bundle of gold ranges from pale to gilded yellows. The perfectly rounded heads and feet and the body, with a touch of paunch, speak for themselves with impressive uniformity.

Touch

The body is often on the softer side of supple, giving this pudgy fellow a fine porosity. The effect may surprise aficionados used to greater rigidity. Nice feel in the hand.

Smell

The fresh, highly floral, round bouquet is consistent from foot to body. The head gives off a subtle waft of green wood. Generous and modern.

Taste

Aromatic and ample from the first puff, with great freshness. Light, highly fragrant woodsy taste dominates the first third; earthy, grilled notes take over in the second. Even at full blast, the freshness holds its own, gaining in roundness. The finale is a tour de force of generosity.

Enjoyment

This temptingly spontaneous, accessible cigar is perfect after a light summer lunch or with an afternoon chocolate treat in the mountains. Sit back and let the goodness sink in.

OVERALL RATING

Strength: 6 ½ – Uniformity: 7 ½ – Character: 8 ½

• In the same family, the **Vegas Robaina Famosos** is equally tasty and nicely balanced.

51

SAINT LUIS REY REGIOS

Length: 5 in. (127 mm)
Ring Gauge: 48 (19.05 mm)
Body: round
Presentation: cabinet of 50, traditional box of 25

Look

An aesthetic experience of roundness itself in the half wheel form. This handsome cigar sports *claro* or *colorado* wrappers.

Touch

The slightly thick texture is silky rather than oily. The supple yet taut body yields generously to the touch. Like all cigars with a slight bulge, the Regios feels great in the hand.

Smell

The initially floral bouquet develops into mild, round spiciness, with a green, vegetal hint.

Taste

The combustion is easy, but the vitola is tricky and requires work before it yields full taste. The slightly harsh beginning notes quickly give way to more woodsy, round aromas, which maintain great freshness to the end.

Enjoyment

This robusto, abetted by the format's popularity in the 1980s, took its place alongside the Romeo y Julieta Exhibición No. 4 and the H. Upmann Connoisseur No. 1. It makes a fine after-lunch smoke if you have an hour to spare.

52

OVERALL RATING

Strength: 7 ½ – Uniformity: 7 – Character: 8

VEGA FINA ROBUSTOS

Length: 4 ⅞ in. (125 mm)
Ring Gauge: 48 (19 mm)
Body: round
Presentation: traditional box of 25

Look

This slightly silky, highly uniform robusto wrapped in *colorado* is perfectly balanced. Its understated white ring bears the initials VF.

Touch

A well-proportioned cigar, it is supple on the outside, with a tantalizing inside. Nicely shaped, with the head's roundness echoing the body's bulge. A fine feel in the hand.

Smell

The mild, aromatic, fresh bouquet is slightly woodsy and short-lived in the nose.

Taste

Like all light structured, predominantly mild cigars, this robusto serves up a balance between taste and smoothness in the first third. A range of quickly fading, woodsy aromas comes out in the second third.

Enjoyment

The Vega Fina makes an enriching contribution to the taste range of the great Robusto family. This accessible cigar treats the palate to a slow, uniform unfolding of flavor that emphasizes the finale's richness. Never overtaxing on the taste buds, this vitola is perfect as an evening's second cigar. It is equally suited for daytime smoking at work, where the fresh, slightly dry aroma should not offend non-smokers.

53

OVERALL RATING
Strength: 6 – Uniformity: 8 ½ – Character: 7 ½

BOLÍVAR ROYAL CORONAS

Length: 4 ⅞ in. (124 mm)
Ring Gauge: 50 (19.84 mm)
Body: square
Presentation: traditional box of 25

Look

This stout, squared-off fellow is instantly recognizable for its sharp angles and early-nineteenth-century ring. The highly consistent form is generally clad in warm *colorado* tones.

Touch

Slightly fleshy and rough to the touch, this robusto leaves behind the fine oily film that is a hallmark of rich, well-made cigars.

Smell

An atypical Bolivar, more sweet-smelling and round than usual. The rather weak scent of the body is marked by leather; that of the foot is grassier and fresher. Both are quick to disappear.

Taste

Physical and present without heaviness, the taste is intensified by rapid, easy combustion. The highly woodsy start gives way to subtle spicy and savory tones. Harmonious and well balanced overall.

Enjoyment

Perfect for a light lunch or a moment's relaxation, the Royal Coronas is a favorite among aficionados who dislike excessive strongness. Have a glass of water on hand for the somewhat dry finale.

OVERALL RATING
Strength: 7 – Uniformity: 6 ½ – Character: 8

COHIBA ROBUSTOS

Length: 4 ⅞ in. (124 mm)
Ring Gauge: 50 (19.84 mm)
Body: round
Presentation: varnished cabinet of 25

Look

With its golden or red earth tobacco, this robusto will stand out in any crowd. The Art Deco ring and the bulging form add to its overall appeal.

Touch

The bundle tempts the hand with rich, unctuous texture and hardy dimensionality. The outstanding suppleness lends elegance to this characteristically more rustic format.

Smell

The distinctive bouquet is generous and aromatic, rich in honeyed spices. Leathery notes, more marked at the head and foot, are borne on an oiled silkiness.

Taste

Rich and full from the start, the flavor blends spices and woodsy taste with great finesse. The ambered, fruity, honeyed notes increase through the final third with a seductive and winning alchemy.

Enjoyment

Despite complaints about its high cost, this brilliant robusto is undoubtedly the stuff of myth. Savor it after a generous dinner with full-bodied wines.

55

OVERALL RATING
Strength: 8 – Uniformity: 8 ½ – Character: 8

JUAN LÓPEZ SELECCIÓN No. 2

Length: 4 ⅞ in. (124 mm)
Ring Gauge: 50 (19.84 mm)
Body: round
Presentation: cabinet of 25

Look

Well-wrapped, at once silky and unctuous, this vitola packs old time "big cigar" allure. Though available in *claro* and *maduro*, it looks best clad in the red tones of *colorado*.

Touch

All around perfection: nice in the hand, thick and smooth to the touch, with a slight softness that becomes it.

Smell

The rich, intense start seems to belong to a very strong cigar, which this robusto is not. The vivid, chocolaty aroma when it's young rounds out into ripe, highly refined leather and pepper tones.

Taste

Easy combustion makes for rapid-fire unfolding of distinct flavor sensations. The pronouncedly vegetal start quickly expands into a half-earthy, half-woodsy register which never overloads the palate. Be careful of drawing too hard, which will cause overheating.

Enjoyment

56

This stunning Havana offers up a virtuoso aromatic panoply in the wink of an eye. You'll almost wish it could last longer. The Selección No. 2 is fine after a meal, and equally good for daytime smoking, where its generous roundness is a real treat.

OVERALL RATING
Strength: 7 – Uniformity: 7 ½ – Character: 9

PARTAGÁS SÉRIE D No. 4

Length: 4 ⅞ in. (124 mm)
Ring Gauge: 50 (19.84 mm)
Body: round
Presentation: unvarnished box of 25

Look

High-strung and muscular, this tubby little aristocrat is most often elegantly wrapped in rich, unctuous *maduro*.

Touch

Pliant rather than supple, silky, and more packed at the foot than in the body.

Smell

A veritable spice rack, the bouquet is immediately vigorous to the point of eliminating cigar newcomers. The round and unctuous notes on a slightly woodsy backdrop are accented with leather and green pepper touches.

Taste

Impeccable combustion delivers the full abundance of flavors, going from fresh to heady spices; from earthy to leathery and underbrush tones. The fast pace is never marred by excess heat. The savory complexity and intensity can overpower inexperienced smokers.

Enjoyment

After a time in the doghouse due to its poorly understood format and uncommon complexity, the D4 has recently regained full honors. This cigar is truly exceptional in richness, consistency, and intoxicating density. It makes an unforgettable after-dinner smoke.

OVERALL RATING

Strength: 9 – Uniformity: 9 ½ – Character: 10

• In the same family, the **Montecristo Millennium 2000**, highly aromatic and expertly crafted, is already a collector's item.

57

RAMÓN ALLONES
SPECIALLY SELECTED

Length: 4 ⅞ in. (124 mm)
Ring Gauge: 50 (19.84 mm)
Body: square
Presentation: traditional box of 25

Look

Lightly tanned and flat-bellied but round at the edges, this cigar bears the mark of determination. Amid the vast available color range, the slightly shiny red and dark brown tones are most becoming.

Touch

The firm body of this jovial vitola is tough, but not too hard. More oily to the touch than its relative the Partagás D4.

Smell

Specially Selected's long-lasting aroma wafts spices on a cacao and caramel background. With proper aging, the honeyed core yields interwoven leather and rich spicy notes.

Taste

This authentic robusto is true to the great tradition, at once rigid and complex. Taste outweighs smell with spices kicking in from the first puffs, which are mixed with round, unctuous, and supremely sensual aromas.

Enjoyment

This epicurean cigar is ideal with southwestern French food, such as fricassee, or long-stewed meats. Too short to go the distance of a great rum, it goes well with a fruity red Burgundy vintage that bears a trace of new wood flavor.

58

OVERALL RATING

Strength: 9 – Uniformity: 8 ½ – Character: 10

ROMEO Y JULIETA
SHORT CHURCHILLS

Length: 4 ⅞ in. (124 mm)
Ring Gauge: 50 (19.84 mm)
Body: square
Presentation: semi-varnished box of 10 or 25; case of 3, with protection tubes

Look

Slightly bronzed, wrapped in very soft and fine caps, this gorgeous and convivial object evokes the dawn of the first days of summer.

Touch

Very soft, with a hint of silk that is an element of its charm. Firm to the touch, this robusto is also supple and extremely regular.

Smell

The faint floral scent is a faithful precursor of what the taste will be like, exhaling notes of a lightly sugared mint tea.

Taste

The Short Churchill is one of those cigars that are gentle on the mouth, easy and light, which do not mark the palate. The linear departure opens with a slight roundness. The ensemble is floral, with evolution throughout taking place in terms of fluidity.

Enjoyment

A cigar for the spring: fresh and aromatic, it is above all very easy to taste, gaily accompanying each moment of the day—and notably cocktail hour, which sets it off remarkably.

59

OVERALL RATING
Strength: 3 – Uniformity: 8 – Character: 9

COHIBA SIGLO V

Length: 6 ⅝ in. (170 mm)
Ring Gauge: 43 (17.07 mm)
Body: round
Presentation: varnished cabinet of 25

Look

With all the upright flare of a British colonial officer of old, this proud beauty is finely cloaked in rich, silky wrappers. To our knowledge, this is the only lonsdale-type cigar available in a cabinet of 25.

Touch

With its finely oiled texture, the Siglo V is as elegant to the touch as to the eye. A certain suppleness only adds to the appeal.

Smell

The generous bouquet is round and floral. The body exudes young leathery scents, while the foot is all mild spice and honeyed vegetal tones. The head breathes out the concentrated aroma typical of Havanas.

Taste

Aromatic richness comes immediately to the fore in heavy floral tones. The complexly refined, spicy blend deepens in the second third, thanks to reliable combustion that never overheats. The youngest of the bunch may be a bit tangy to the taste.

Enjoyment

This cigar is at its best aged: with proper maturation, it is elegance incarnate. Perfect after a fine meal, or for an afternoon with a good book.

OVERALL RATING
Strength: 8 – Uniformity: 8 ½ – Character: 9

LA GLORIA CUBANA MÉDAILLE D'OR No. 2

Length: 6 ⅝ in. (170 mm)
Ring Gauge: 43 (17.07 mm)
Body: round
Presentation: semi-varnished box of 25

Look

This dalia mixes the material richness of a churchill with the lonsdale's elegant format. Generally golden but occasionally deep *colorado* in hue, with an elegant 8-9-8 presentation that brings to mind the Partagás 8-9-8 Varnished Cabinet Selection.

Touch

No softy, the Médaille d'Or No. 2 is a firm and highly-structured cigar that sometimes borders on over-packing. The unctuous tobacco is refined and top quality.

Smell

The luscious, deep gingerbread aroma—more underbrush than unctuous in tone—sets this vitola apart from its Partagás 8-9-8 counterpart.

Taste

Strength mitigated with richness and presence. From the start, ripe woodsy and spiced flavor comes to the fore. This pedigree vitola then mounts to intoxicating heights before delivering a punch with the finale.

Enjoyment

With its mix of unctuous mildness and potency, this fine cigar is the crowning jewel to an elegant dining experience. Its range may overpower inexperienced palates.

OVERALL RATING

Strength: 9 – Uniformity: 8 – Character: 8 ½

• *In the same family, the aforementioned **Partagás 8-9-8 Varnished Cabinet Selection** is intoxicating. **Ditto for the Partagás de Partagás No. 1**, with great classic strength.*

61

PARTAGÁS 8-9-8 VERNI

Length: 6 ¾ in. (170 mm)
Ring Gauge: 43 (17.07 mm)
Body: round
Presentation: varnished cabinet of 25

Look

The presentation in three rows of 8, 9, and 8 cigars was created by Partagás for this product before being borrowed by Ramón Allones and La Gloria Cubana. It is here set off by *colorado-maduro* and *colorado-claro* tobacco leaves.

Touch

Handling the bunch of cigars without breaking it is a perilous feat, but keeping the cigar in your hand is a pleasure: its unctuousness and silkiness are immediately captivating.

Smell

While the body exhales an acidulousness that is definitely present, it is at the foot that its aromas are at their most subtle. There, it deploys a blend of spices and animal leather that should evolve within a few years towards a vintage with gingerbread scents.

Taste

The richness here resides in the spices, which evolve from the freshness of the first curls of smoke towards the unctuousness of the second third, before finishing on warmer overtones. The remarkable blend of classic and exotic tastes can become chaotic if the cigar has been stored poorly.

Enjoyment

A real tenor of the group, always true to form. This great classic from the 1960s has succeeded in regenerating its circle of followers. Sitting less well with light cooking, this is a cigar to follow a hearty meal. Beware, it can be tiring: taste it when you are at your best.

OVERALL RATING
Strength: 9 – Uniformity: 7 ½ – Character: 9

BOLÍVAR LONSDALES

Length: 6½ in. (165 mm)
Ring Gauge: 42 (16.67 mm)
Body: square
Presentation: semi-varnished box of 25

Look

Very elegant and faithful to the tradition of the Cervantes, the Bolívar displays a clear style, in predominantly *maduro* tobacco leaves that confer upon it an undeniable austerity.

Touch

The touch is defined in three words: unctuous, supple, and firm. The unctuousness of rich tobacco, the suppleness of its makeup, the firmness from head to foot, in a regular and homogenous construction.

Smell

Undergrowth and old leather mingle with wet earth in an alluring ensemble. This complexity is the stamp of this cigar, faint and linear along its body. Its aromas are strong as soon as the foot is lit, giving the cigar a scent evocative of an English club.

Taste

While the spice does not manifest itself until the second third, the first third liberates woodsy, unctuous, and humid tastes. Slow and regular combustion makes a distinctive marker for each step. Be careful of the finish, which, though very harmonious, has a tendency to suddenly invade the palate.

Enjoyment

Among the "old-style" cigars, the Lonsdales is worthwhile, especially when accompanied by an aged rum or vintage porto, after lunch.

63

OVERALL RATING
Strength: 7 ½ – Uniformity: 8 – Character: 7

PARTAGÁS LONSDALES
CABINET SELECTION

Length: 6½ in. (165 mm)
Ring Gauge: 42 (16.67 mm)
Body: round
Presentation: cabinet of 50, traditional box of 25

Look

The cabinet selection's gorgeous half wheel is clad in golden tones of fiery earth that deepen with age. The heads are so well-rounded that they seem closer to art than to reality.

Touch

The well-constructed cigar is firm to the point of being packed and feels good in the hand. Finely wrapped and stylish, it is neither silky nor oily.

Smell

In young cigars, the scent is rather harsh and astringent. With time, this gives way to deeper, cacao aromas that build to the spicy strength for which Partagás are known.

Taste

Ample woodsy and peppery flavor tantalizes the palate from the start. With smoking, the strong, woodsy character expands to grace each and every taste bud. The finale is a spiced medley.

Enjoyment

Beware: while the cigars improve with age in the cabinet selection, those in the boxed version seem to suffer from arrested development. At its best, this lonsdale goes hand in hand with great wines. Alternate between puffs and sips for an almost religious experience.

OVERALL RATING

Strength: 9 – Uniformity: 6 – Character: 8 ½

• In the same family, the **Saint Luis Rey Lonsdales Cabinet Selection** is stronger and less spiced.

RAFAEL GONZÁLEZ LONSDALES

Length: 6 ⅜ in. (165 mm)
Ring Gauge: 42 (16.67 mm)
Body: square
Presentation: traditional box of 25

Look

This great classic is perfectly elegant, elongated, and well-built at once. The squared cut is highly becoming, especially in burnished gold tones.

Touch

Firm and packed, this cigar is a favorite among lovers of taut rigidity.

Smell

The nearly feminine bouquet, with its lovely floral notes, has no trace of spice. A green accent lends freshness.

Taste

The smooth, enchantingly subtle start opens into fresh aromas of mixed, delicate spices on a round, leathery backdrop from which continual unctuous intimations make you forget the slow combustion.

Enjoyment

This inspirational, imaginative, and creative vitola goes well with a good book or a musical interlude. It is fine food for thought. The aromas never overpower the palate; on the contrary, they augment its discernment. Savor the cigar after a seafood meal or following a delicious winter snack of cake and hot tea.

OVERALL RATING

Strength: 7 ½ – Uniformity: 8 – Character: 9

• In the same family, **the El Rey del Mundo Lonsdales** is milder.

65

SANCHO PANZA MOLINOS

Length: 6 ½ in. (165 mm)
Ring Gauge: 42 (16.67 mm)
Body: square
Presentation: traditional box of 25

Look

The box has changed, with jolly Sancho no longer pictured on the side. But the cigar remains its well-constructed self, available in a wide range of colors and ringed with an elegant brown oval band.

Touch

Straight as an arrow, this cigar is nowadays packed to the point of rigidity, but retains a hint of suppleness when well executed. The slightly rough, grainy texture accentuates its austere allure.

Smell

Now the subtle bouquet is vegetal and green, without the interruption of any strong spices. This aromatic restructuring goes hand in hand with the new presentation.

Taste

The start is on light vegetal notes, with a touch of astringency. Only when it reaches the perfect temperature does the Molinos serve up its richer, more woodsy flavor. The intense last third may tend to overheat, due to its tight packing. It must be slowly savored, with pauses when it lags or races.

Enjoyment

Long-ignored, this cervantes has won praise for its richness and charm. Hopefully the new version will be equally pleasing, for example accompanying a meal served with a fine, tannic wine.

OVERALL RATING

Strength: 7 – Uniformity: 6 ½ – Character: 6 ½

66

COHIBA SIGLO III

Length: 6 ⅛ in. (155 mm)
Ring Gauge: 42 (16.67 mm)
Body: round
Presentation: varnished cabinet of 25

Look

These handsome vitolas are well-structured, with uniformly round heads. Whether slightly longer looking in the cabinet presentation or seemingly more abbreviated in the boxed version, the Siglo III is invariably appealing.

Touch

Consistent and packed without too much firmness, this cigar is elegant to the touch.

Smell

The first puffs release memories of fields, farms, and bucolic expanses, with the slightly heavy whiff of wet earth on summer mornings. The head is more leathery, while the body has a non-matte powdery aroma. The foot exudes floral notes mixed with a gingerbread scent.

Taste

Packed and therefore slow, this corona's first third heats the body to its perfect cruising speed. It then turns savory, quickly moving from dry notes to round spiciness. Proper aging transforms the strength into a uniquely delicate, honeyed richness.

Enjoyment

Few cigars in this format offer up such refinement. A few years after its creation, the Siglo III's impressive progress is to be admired.

OVERALL RATING
Strength: 7 ½ – Uniformity: 8 – Character: 9

• In the same family, the **Partagás 8-9-8 Cabinet Selection** (unvarnished) is more matte and long-lined.

LA GLORIA CUBANA SABROSOS

Length: 6 ⅛ in. (155 mm)
Ring Gauge: 42 (16.67 mm)
Body: square
Presentation: traditional box of 25

Look

This impressively uniform gran corona, with its lonsdale airs, comes wrapped in hues from *claro* to *maduro*, by way of the red nuances of light *colorado*. The round head is artfully crafted.

Touch

Highly consistent, supple and sensitive but rarely too tight, the Sabrosos's classy looks are sustained by its fine quality tobacco.

Smell

The simple, direct, matter-of-fact bouquet speaks for authentic Havana tradition. Mild floral scents are borne on heavier, slightly pepper notes.

Taste

This classic iconoclast opens on refined aromas that quickly build in strength on rich, unctuous honeyed and pepper flavors. The good combustion assures a certain persistent freshness.

Enjoyment

Its top-quality tobacco, uniformity, and good value make the Sabrosos a cigar to be reckoned with. It is accessible even to inexperienced smokers.

OVERALL RATING

Strength: 7 – Uniformity: 8 – Character: 7

• In the same family, the **Romeo y Julieta Coronas Grandes** is more straightforward.

HOYO DE MONTERREY
LE HOYO DES DIEUX

Length: 6 ⅛ in. (155 mm)
Ring Gauge: 42 (16.67 mm)
Body: round
Presentation: cabinet of 50 or 25

Look

With its beautiful half wheel of 50 presentation—preferable to the cabinet of 25 for extended aging—this cigar does not show its forty years. Its youthful complexion is rarely darker than a gold tone, with a fine, silky texture.

Touch

At once supple and tensed, with a risk of tightness that makes it a bit hard sometimes, the Hoyo des Dieux is smooth, oiled, and silky to the touch. The bundle has a pleasing heft, and the cigar feels at home in the hand.

Smell

In keeping with Le Hoyo tradition, the bouquet is preponderantly floral, with persistent underbrush tones providing an element of variation.

Taste

The mild, round start expands with sweeter, deeper aromas in the second third. The finale brings out unctuous vegetal tonalities.

Enjoyment

Those looking for robusto-style bounty may consider this Hoyo a lightweight. However, it makes a lasting impression in the traditional taste range of cacao, wood, musk, and spices. The Hoyo des Dieux is fine after lunch with a young wine. Its balance and uniform, easy combustion also make it a good daytime choice.

OVERALL RATING
Strength: 7 – Uniformity: 8 – Character: 7 ½

69

PARTAGÁS CORONAS
CABINET SELECTION

Length: 5½ in. (142 mm)
Ring Gauge: 42 (16.67 mm)
Body: round
Presentation: cabinet of 50, traditional box of 25

Look

With the noble severity of a true corona, this handsome cigar dons generally gold colorings, with an occasional *maduro*.

Touch

Slightly velvety but not silky, thanks to the oils within. The firm body is supple but never soft, unless damaged by humidity, which proves its downfall.

Smell

The typically Partagás scent is a mix of woodsy and spicy with a wild finale, especially in the young cigar. Maturation, especially in the cabinet, lends subtlety.

Taste

In keeping with Partagás tradition the Coronas Cabinet Selection has a certain strictness, with bold coffee, cacao, musk, and spiced aromas that start strong and last long.

Enjoyment

This handsome, somewhat austere cigar has built up a loyal following over the years. More fully developed in the cabinet version, its complex aromatic texture is the stuff of a superior vintage. Savored after an ordinary lunch, its slow, uniform combustion will never tire an experienced smoker.

OVERALL RATING

Strength: 9 – Uniformity: 9 – Character: 8 ½

• *In the same family, the **Juan López Coronas** is equally strict, but milder and less spicy in the mouth.*

ROMEO Y JULIETA CORONAS

Length: 5 ½ in. (142 mm)
Ring Gauge: 42 (16.67 mm)
Body: square
Presentation: traditional box of 25

Look

This great classic is all poise and pedigree, with perfectly balanced construction, a handsome traditional ring, and tonalities ranging from light to barely dark brown.

Touch

The supple, silky body is perfectly porous and bred to obey.

Smell

The bouquet sets out on a highly vegetal trail, then turns slightly acidulous, nearly sharp. The body brings out reassuringly traditional leathery notes, moving into a soothing finale.

Taste

True to its alluring self and not to preconceptions, this accessible, companionable corona serves up a smooth and round floral flavor in keeping with today's tastes. Twenty years ago, this vitola was rich and strong but changed to cultivate a following among lovers of smoother cigars with easy combustion that demands much less effort.

Enjoyment

This cigar's adaptation to current taste is a success story. It makes a fine friend at work for daytime smoking. Faithful followers will savor its fresh yet stable flavor anytime, anywhere.

OVERALL RATING

Strength: 6 ½ – Uniformity: 7 – Character: 7 ½

• In the same family, the **Diplomáticos No. 3** is a traditional cigar that has made quite a comeback in recent years.

71

SANCHO PANZA CORONAS

Length: 5 ½ in. (142 mm)
Ring Gauge: 42 (16.67 mm)
Body: square
Presentation: traditional box of 25

Look

Uniform as a military parade, the handsomely squared body comes clad in hues running from *claro* to *colorado*. Its austere elegance is softened by the round head and embellished by its brown oval ring.

Touch

Though slightly packed, this cigar is supple to the touch and rigid on the palm. Its unctuous, slightly shiny wrapper lends a smooth, silky touch.

Smell

At the foot, the initial woodsy scent dissolves in vegetal nuances. The body exudes a hint of new leather that gives an overall appeal.

Taste

The first third is played in mild floral tones, while the second takes a tannic, woodsy turn. The finale deploys rich, heavy underbrush aromas with lime and coffee overtones.

Enjoyment

A great classic in the format, the Sancho Panza Coronas falls somewhere between Partagás richness and the Hoyo du Roi's mildness. Try it after lunch, without alcohol, to give its flavor your undivided attention.

OVERALL RATING

Strength: 6 ½ – Uniformity: 8 – Character: 7 ½

• In the same family, the **Punch Coronas** are admirably consistent.

72

VEGAS ROBAINA FAMILIARES

Length: 5 ⅝ in. (142 mm)
Ring Gauge: 42 (16.67 mm)
Body: square
Presentation: semi-varnished box of 25

Look

Presentation is not its strongest asset: dark caps give it a dry and strong appearance that does not tally with reality.

Touch

To the touch, the Familiares combines coarseness and smoothness, elegance and distinction: it is a pleasure to hold. At times, a slight tightness of the body may lead to a slow combustion.

Smell

At first whiff, the bouquet is not particularly generous, dominated by fairly discreet young leather notes. But with a little patience, you can discover more rustic scents reminiscent of a rainy summer day.

Taste

This classic and elegant corona develops a slow burning, which effectively underlines its humid-wood aromas, without ever falling into aggression. While this is not a range of powerful spices, its heightened flavors linger on the palate.

Enjoyment

The corona is doubtless the least well known of the models of the brand—the pirámide and the robusto are more successful—which does not mean that it is not worth savoring. An excellent afternoon cigar for accompanying a coffee or a spot of reading.

OVERALL RATING

Strength: 5 ½ – Uniformity: 7 – Character: 8

73

TRINIDAD COLONIALES

Length: 5 ¼ in. (132 mm)
Ring Gauge: 44 (17.46 mm)
Body: round
Presentation: varnished presentation box of 24;
case of 5

Look

In this presentation box worthy of a jewelry collection, the bunches of cigars are ribbon-bound. When the box is opened, each tier appears like the layer of a sumptuous *millefeuille* that makes up the ensemble.

Touch

Generally very silky, the Coloniales is comfortable to hold, while remaining discreet. The great homogeneity of its construction is extremely appreciable.

Smell

A blend of woodiness and young leather, the bouquet masks the spices, producing very enticing aromas. Cedar leaves in the presentation box shade the unheated perfumes when you take a cigar from the box, but, shortly after, this influence becomes inconspicuous.

Taste

An unctuous licorice predominates here, with a regular combustion that distinctly marks the passage of the different steps. A gentle beginning, a round mid-course, and a powerful finish. The aromas remain very elegant throughout the three thirds.

Enjoyment

The Coloniales stands apart from the usual petit coronas: more elegant than most of them, it is an excellent post-lunch cigar for occasional lovers and a daytime cigar for confirmed lovers. Highly consistent, it rarely disappoints.

74

OVERALL RATING
Strength: 6 ½ – Uniformity: 8 ½ – Character: 9

MONTECRISTO PETIT EDMUNDOS

Length: 4 ⅜ in. (110 mm)
Ring Gauge: 52 (20.64 mm)
Body: round
Presentation: unvarnished box of 10 or 25

Look

What the baguette is to Paris, the Petit Edmundos is to Havana. Presented like large barley sugars, these cigars are among the most appetizing available, dressed in dark or light colors that underline their *sympatonique* quality.

Touch

Filling the hand with its generous roundness, the Petit Edmundos is a silky, unctuous cigar. Its full belly makes it agreeable to roll between the fingers. Though short on elegance, it commands the lover's caress.

Smell

Rich and powerful, it offers the nose an immediate presence. Its animal and amber overtones give an idea of what it will taste like.

Taste

Be careful, there is nothing light about this little fellow: on the contrary, from the first curls of smoke, it directly knocks a punch, in peppery tannic overtones that it maintains to the finish. Due to the size-to-diameter proportion, evolution in taste is almost nonexistent, but the richness largely compensates for size, offering ample satisfaction.

Enjoyment

The Petit Edmundos joins the tasty cigars of this renowned family. Excellent after a fine meal of fish or meat, cooked in traditional style or otherwise, it is a cigar for serious lovers, who will find in it a perfect daytime companion. Take care, however, not to over-indulge—its size and easy burning could well lead you in this direction—and spoil the pleasure of this treat.

75

OVERALL RATING
Strength: 9 – Uniformity: 9 – Character: 9 ½

HOYO DE MONTERREY
PETIT ROBUSTOS

Length: 4 in. (102 mm)
Ring Gauge: 50 (19.84 mm)
Body: round
Presentation: cabinet of 25; case of 3

Look

Small in size and fairly round in diameter, the Petit Robustos is nonetheless a heavy charmer that the eye will appreciate. Dressed in shades ranging from *colorado* to *claro*, it is the sole example of this format presented in a cabinet.

Touch

First of all, the bunch can nestle in the hollow of your palm, next comes the cigar, which seems to disappear into your hand. It is as discreet to the touch as it is pronounced to the palate.

Smell

We rediscover the floral style of Hoyo: round and mellow, with hidden woodsy aromas. The bouquet, fairly linear, does not show any evolution—because of its compactness.

Taste

The initial taste is mellower than that of its Montecristo counterpart. Its charm is found in the draw, which offers, from the outset, a multitude of aromas. An accumulation of notably hazelnut and licorice notes makes its presence felt on the palate, in remarkable fashion. This is a high-performance cigar, as rich as it is pleasant, with an extraordinarily fluid tempo, without any marked progression along the three thirds—as they are spaced so closely next to one another.

Enjoyment

This half robusto is pure pleasure. Ideal for pre-dinner drinks or after lunch, or else a second evening cigar for serious lovers. Take care, however, not to be taken in by its lures and to over-consume—this would spoil the pleasure.

OVERALL RATING
Strength: 7 – Uniformity: 8 ½ – Character: 9 ½

76

BOLÍVAR PETIT CORONAS CABINET SELECTION

Length: 5 ⅛ in. (129 mm)
Ring Gauge: 42 (16.67 mm)
Body: round
Presentation: cabinet of 50, traditional box of 25

Look

The bundle of round, well-made coronas is a gem of uniformity and consistency.

Touch

Smooth, firm, and taut without being too tight, this cigar feels great in the hand. Hold the bundle to your ear: you can almost hear it breathe.

Smell

The alluring bouquet is round, fresh, and tonic. Wet-earth notes, initially subdued in the body, are more ample at the foot and head.

Taste

The earthy, slightly pungent first third builds almost to bitterness before yielding to mild spices in the last third. The overall impression is unctuous and consistent, with a fine balance between force and taste that is long-lasting in the mouth.

Enjoyment

Though this petit corona cannot pack the complexity of a torpedo or churchill, its aromatic range is one of the format's most fascinating. It goes well with a meal for the occasional aficionado and makes a good daytime cigar for the experienced Havana lover. A strong little chap with indubitable taste.

OVERALL RATING

Strength: 6 – Uniformity: 7 ½ – Character: 8

• In the same family, the **Romeo y Julieta Petit Coronas** is more earthy than spicy.

COHIBA SIGLO II

Length: 5 ½ in. (129 mm)
Ring Gauge: 42 (16.67 mm)
Body: round
Presentation: varnished cabinet of 25

Look

The homogeneous little bundle of 25 coronas ranges in hue from golden to deep red tones, with perfectly rounded heads.

Touch

Supremely silky with an almost sponge-like touch, the firm, well-made cigar feels right in the hand.

Smell

The floral bouquet, with its leather and woodsy overtones, has an overall touch of pleasing moistness. Short-lived in the nose and devoid of spices, this cigar makes an excellent vintage, with pronounced Madera aromas highly divergent from its youthful incarnation.

Taste

The short and easy burn-time (no more than fifty minutes) offers up tastes in rapid succession. Floral notes give way to morning spices, then vegetal thickness. The second third builds gently to the finale's full array.

Enjoyment

Don't give in to the path of least resistance and smoke this cigar too quickly. Its rich aromas merit slower savoring. Tasty and structured, the Siglo II goes well with a simple meal or finishes it off in style with an excellent arabica coffee.

OVERALL RATING

Strength: 7 – Uniformity: 8 ½ – Character: 7 ½

• In the same family, the **Juan López Petit Coronas** is milder, with a squared body.

HOYO DE MONTERREY
LE HOYO DU PRINCE

Length: 5 ⅛ in. (130 mm)
Ring Gauge: 40 (15.87 mm)
Body: round
Presentation: cabinet of 25

Look

Understated, with no exterior signs of richness, the lovely bunch of petit coronas is a bundle of fine uniformity, in handsome golden tones, never too oily.

Touch

This thoroughly elegant cigar has a fine, silky texture. A bit overwhelming when packed too tight, its slim shape sometimes feels lost in the hand.

Smell

The bouquet is mild, floral, understated, and short-lived. The body is vegetal in aroma, with no trace of bitterness or pushiness.

Taste

From its finely aromatic, slightly mild start, the smooth cigar gains richness and presence in the second third before entering into full force for the finale of green pepper flavor tinged with cacao tones. Some risk of overheating, which is an unpleasant result of tightness.

Enjoyment

This cigar is better in the company of food or drink than all alone. It can be enjoyed at any time of day, thanks to its easy combustion and is particularly nice with an afternoon coffee on the way back to work following a light lunch.

79

OVERALL RATING

Strength: 6 – Uniformity: 6 ½ – Character: 6 ½

• In the same family, the **Sancho Panza Non Plus**, a mareva, has a more matte flavor.

PARTAGÁS PETIT CORONAS
CABINET SELECTION

Length: 5 ⅛ in. (129 mm)
Ring Gauge: 42 (16.67 mm)
Body: round
Presentation: cabinet of 50, traditional box of 25

Look

The handsome half wheel of petit coronas, with their nicely rounded heads and feet, shows off the format's classic balance. The color range runs from deeper claro to light *colorado*, by way of ocher shades.

Touch

With no apparent oiliness, this cigar leaves a smooth, slightly grainy whisper in the hand. In the cabinet selection, this vitola is uniformly porous and supple from foot to head.

Smell

Fresh, vegetal, and short-lived. The young cigar's acidulous hints turn more woodsy, without forfeiting the vegetal base.

Taste

Generous from the first, the woodsy, slightly sugared aromas lend a special dimensionality. The bold final third rekindles in spice. Aging merely hones its profile and mellows its style.

Enjoyment

This regal petit corona is straightforward, honest, and fits in everywhere, from a light lunch to a simple dinner topped with cognac, daily errands or a contemplative break therefrom. That is, provided you are acquainted with intoxicating Havanas.

OVERALL RATING

Strength: 8 ½ – Uniformity: 9 ½ – Character: 9

• *In the same family, the **H. Upmann No. 4** is equally well-made and easy-going.*

POR LARRAÑAGA PETIT CORONAS CABINET SELECTION

Length: 5 ⅛ in. (129 mm)
Ring Gauge: 42 (16.67 mm)
Body: round
Presentation: cabinet of 50

Look

With the beauty of stripped-down simplicity, this gold-toned petit corona has a hint of crusty country bread to it. The round head and feet and the harmonious body are mighty appealing.

Touch

Supple but not quite soft, this understated cigar feels fine in the hand. Its silky texture is smooth rather than oily, with more firmness in the body and head than at the foot.

Smell

The bouquet's enticing scent whets the appetite, starting with fresh floral notes on a slightly woodsy ground and building to new leather tones in the body, with no hint of dryness or powder.

Taste

It deserves to be smoked young for its freshness, roundness, and tonicity. A slight fruitiness gives it a blithe tone that marks the beginning, while the last third is full of strong, abundant, lush aroma.

Enjoyment

This delicious petit corona is a well-kept secret worth discovering. It is highly adaptable, fine for daytime and after meals alike, and ideal for the gourmand who has no time or wish to dig into a bigger format but relishes a flexible, ever-accessible smoke.

OVERALL RATING

Strength: 6 ½ – Uniformity: 9 ½ – Character: 9 ½

• In the same family: the **Diplomáticos No. 4**, with stronger leathery aromas.

81

PUNCH PETIT CORONAS

Length: 5 ⅛ in. (129 mm)
Ring Gauge: 42 (16.67 mm)
Body: round
Presentation: cabinet of 50, traditional box of 25
(Punch Petit Coronas del Punch)

Look

The compact, uniform bunch, with its greenish brown, slightly matte tones comes bound in a yellow ribbon.

Touch

More unctuous and smooth than silky, this supple vitola is somewhat crackling on the inside but never dry, with a solid feel in the hand, unusual for this format.

Smell

Pure Punch. Earthy and moist, with a grassy vegetal foot in the young cigar. The body becomes more ambered, developed, and round with time. This cigar speaks loud and clear, with insistently rich, wet-earth aroma.

Taste

Superior combustion releases the ripe, earthy, nonspicy flavor with exponential impact. Honeyed, leather, and underbrush tones are equally present. The finale is strong and intense.

Enjoyment

Easy yet tasty, this cigar mixes well. For Punch aficionados, it comes in handy after a light dinner and is also fine for work or a contemplative break.

OVERALL RATING
Strength: 8 – Uniformity: 9 – Character: 8 ½

PUNCH ROYAL SELECTION No. 12

Length: 5 ⅛ in. (129 mm)
Ring Gauge: 42 (16.67 mm)
Body: round
Presentation: cabinet of 25

Look

The compact bundle, with its gold to burnished tones, is elegance itself.

Touch

The bundle is a heavyweight for its format, with a nice heft in the hand. The packed, oiled body makes a fine overall impression.

Smell

The rich, wet-earth aroma—a signature of great Punch models—has a grassy touch that blends well with the body's soft leather notes. Depending on the year, this cigar may tend to show more acidulous, vegetal scents.

Taste

Real Punch with a direct explosiveness in the mouth, the earthy flavor opens in a woodsy, spiced register with cacao hints. The overall balance is winning.

Enjoyment

Despite its somewhat sluggish combustion due to density, this mareva is mighty pleasing. Passing irregularity is not to be confused with inconsistency here, as the touch of suspense only adds to the fun. With its generous roundness, the Royal Selection No. 12 is nice after a light lunch or for afternoon smoking.

OVERALL RATING

Strength: 7 – Uniformity: 6 ½ – Character: 6 ½

• In the same family, the **H. Upmann Petit Coronas** is more classic, with a more linear taste range.

83

RAFAEL GONZÁLEZ
PETIT CORONAS

Length: 5 ⅛ in. (129 mm)
Ring Gauge: 42 (16.67 mm)
Body: square
Presentation: traditional box of 25

Look

With its generally *maduro* tones blending with the ring color, this cigar's no-nonsense looks are emphasized by its rectilinear profile.

Touch

The thick, oiled tobacco is densely packed through and through, giving an edge of seriousness to the touch. The handsome, perfectly uniform wrapper is a fine result of limited, painstaking production.

Smell

The highly vegetal start has a second wave of spiced aroma, which is typically short-lived in the nose.

Taste

The initial spiced flavors of wood and leather quickly build the peppery, tannic taste. Density has a hand in the rapid crescendo, which can border on overheating and overpower an inexperienced palate.

Enjoyment

Not to be confused with the Petit Lonsdales of the same brand, which are excellent but less potent, this petit corona is perfect for European and American cuisine. It is equally fine with a before-dinner drink, at the end of the day, or as a second evening smoke.

OVERALL RATING

Strength: 8 ½ – Uniformity: 7 – Character: 7

• In the same family, the **Diplomáticos No. 4** is less strong and more floral.

TRINIDAD REYES

Length: 4 ⅜ in. (110 mm)
Ring Gauge: 40 (15.87 mm)
Body: round
Presentation: varnished presentation box
of 12 or 24; case of 5

Look

The varnished box presentation suggests a small box of
sweets. The size-to-diameter proportion is well
balanced. The golden hues, heightened with a touch of
gloss, are an invitation to succumb. Slightly thinner than
the Partagás Shorts, the Reyes is also more elegant.

Touch

Astonishingly agreeable to hold for a small format, it stands out for its suppleness and
silkiness.

Smell

Spring makes an appearance in the humidor. A blend of floral freshness and gentle
woodsy spices, the subtle and restrained scent is an invitation to go further. It is at the
foot that the bouquet fills out.

Taste

From beginning to end, we remain on a highly aromatic tempo, rich in woodiness but
without pronounced notes of spiciness, helping the cigar to burn easily all the way through.
Always round in flavor, this generous cigar provides a slightly unctuous and salty finish.

Enjoyment

A mountain source at the height of summer. The Reyes is a delectable daytime cigar to
taste with a coffee, a tea, or, even better, a pre-dinner drink. Beware, however, of its
accessibility, which can easily trap the lover. Otherwise said, better not to drink too often
at the source—its price will help you restrain yourself.

OVERALL RATING

Strength: 5 – Uniformity: 9 – Character: 8 ½

PARTAGÁS SHORTS

Length: 4 ⅜ in. (110 mm)
Ring Gauge: 42 (16.67 mm)
Body: round
Presentation: cabinet of 50, traditional box of 25

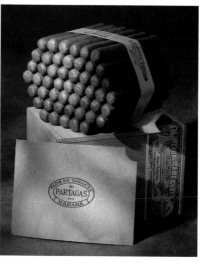

Look

This brilliantly constructed, golden-toned bundle, with its fine silky textures has the precision and alignment of a perfect log cabin. The cabinet selection is incomparable.

Touch

The unctuous, oiled body is pleasingly firm, with no risk of overheating in combustion.

Smell

The generous spring bouquet, at once fresh and round, builds along floral lines. A tiny leather hint brings out a touch of tannic character.

Taste

With an aromatic complexity unusual for this format, the Shorts delivers fresh, round vegetal flavor mixed with spices and vanilla wood in the first third along with leather, honey, coffee, and other flavors in the second. The bold finale is spicy. Long-lasting in the mouth.

Enjoyment

An excellent accompaniment, this cigar is a perfect spokesman for the new millennium's taste requirements. It doesn't overwhelm the atmosphere and takes just twenty minutes to smoke. It is equally good with a beer, coffee, or light lunch, or when smoked during a summer's afternoon spent outdoors.

OVERALL RATING

Strength: 8 – Uniformity: 9 ½ – Character: 9

• In the same family, the **Diplomáticos No. 5** is more squared and lighter in flavor.

RAMÓN ALLONES
SMALL CLUB CORONAS

Length: 4 ⅛ in. (110 mm)
Ring Gauge: 42 (16.67 mm)
Body: square
Presentation: traditional box of 25

Look

Though its shortness may keep it from standing out from other cigars, the Small Club is to be admired for its superior uniformity and size-to-diameter proportions. This homogeneous cigar comes clad in consummate *colorado*.

Touch

The unctuous texture ranges from thick to grainy depending on manufacturing. The ring size makes for a good feel in the hand. Aficionados who like to keep their cigar between their lips will like its fit in the mouth.

Smell

The short-lived bouquet is no main selling point here. The slightly earthy, non-spicy scent is distinguished only by an understated, silky roundness.

Taste

The excellent burning quality lets the full and intense flavors show off their woodsy notes, which take on increasingly unctuous and exotic layerings that last in the mouth. Warning: the final burst of power may surprise you, but its impact is short-lived.

Enjoyment

This small format cigar fits right between the index finger and thumb, to hide in the palm. The Small Club makes for easy smoking on all occasions and is perfect for initiating occasional aficionados into the realms of greater aromatic complexity.

87

OVERALL RATING

Strength: 7 – Uniformity: 8 – Character: 8

• In the same family, the **Punch Petit Punch** is a great representative of the new generation of small format cigars.

SAN CRISTÓBAL DE LA HABANA
EL PRÍNCIPE

Length: 4 ⅛ in. (110 mm)
Ring Gauge: 42 (16.67 mm)
Body: square
Presentation: traditional box of 25

Look

With their candy-box presentation, these silky little *colorado* cigars have a winning air. The cigar seems to grow a bit once the large and somewhat odd, gothic-inspired ring is removed.

Touch

The highly supple El Príncipe is so manageable that it can get lost in the hand. Smooth, soft wrappers encase the oiled, squared off, and pleasingly pliant body. Play with it a bit before lighting to enjoy the palpable moistness.

Smell

The body exudes a subtle floral, slightly woodsy, fresh scent. The overall effect is alluring but so short-lived that it has to be sniffed several times to really be perceived.

Taste

This modern cigar is easy, rapid, light, not spicy, and aromatic. It is suited for any moment of a busy day, delivering forty minutes' worth of unctuous, delicately woodsy, generous, and intense flavor.

Enjoyment

Though the first puffs don't quite pay off, you'll wish it would never end once the flavor kicks in. Its lightness makes it a good after-dinner cigar for occasional smokers. It is also a fine morning choice for experienced aficionados.

OVERALL RATING

Strength: 5 ½ – Uniformity: 8 – Character: 8 ½

• In the same family try the **Romeo y Julieta Petit Princess** *(4 in. [102 mm], ring gauge 40 [15.87 mm])*.

COHIBA LANCEROS

Length: 7 ½ in. (192 mm)
Ring Gauge: 38 (15.08 mm)
Body: round
Presentation: semi-varnished box of 25

Look

The elegant box opens on a jewel-like alignment of dignified cigars. The round foot, twisted head, and slim body exude 1960s style.

Touch

This aristocrat's silky texture and overall refined uniformity voluptuously stretch out in the palm of the hand.

Smell

Rich and strong in its heyday, the Lanceros is now more understated, almost mild, in a vegetal and lightly floral morning register.

Taste

After a subtle start, the second third is rich and physical. Cacao aromas, brought out by touches of licorice and spice, tickle the palate. Beware: defective fabrication can cause excess strength and overheating.

Enjoyment

A star of yesteryear, the Lanceros is unjustly forgotten today. When the fashion changes again, aficionados will rediscover its magnificent refinement. Female smokers may also help it out of its obscurity. An after-dinner cigar for the long evenings when time comes to a standstill and the philosopher in you comes out.

OVERALL RATING

Strength: 7 ½ – Uniformity: 8 ½ – Character: 7

• In the same family, the **Vegueros No. 1** is consistently vegetal from end to end.

89

TRINIDAD FUNDADORES

Length: 7 ¼ in. (192 mm)
Ring Gauge: 38 (15.08 mm)
Body: round
Presentation: unvarnished box of 50 or 24

Look

Slender and spindled, with its head topped in a knot, this elegant cigar is most attractive young, before its *colorado* tones deepen. With time, the surface oils fade and the gold ring rusts to bronze.

Touch

Elegant and supple almost to the point of softness, this cigar is a joy in the hand, to be tasted on the palm before the palate.

Smell

Initially understated, the aroma unleashes woodsy floral body notes with a mix of new leather. The foot is rich, savory, and lightly ambered.

Taste

Due to its size, the Fundadores starts slow and mild, building with heat to an impressive spiced range with a touch of pepper now and then. The subtle second third leads to an alluring finale that finishes off with slightly spicy notes.

Enjoyment

While most of the great brands concentrated on robustos in the 1990s, Trinidad focused on this unique format. The Fundadores makes an excellent vintage and is perfect after a great meal with rich, deep wines.

OVERALL RATING

Strength: 8 ½ – Uniformity: 9 – Character: 9 ½

• In the same family, the **Partagás Série du Connoisseur No. 1** starts off stronger and is spicier in aroma.

LA GLORIA CUBANA MÉDAILLE D'OR No. 1

Length: 7 ¼ in. (185 mm)
Ring Gauge: 36 (14.29 mm)
Body: round
Presentation: semi-varnished box of 25

Look

This gran panatela is a handsome long-line cigar, generally clad in *claro* and occasionally in *maduro* hues.

Touch

More soft than supple, this cigar doesn't feel its size in the hand. The slightly unctuous tobacco leaves a fine film on the skin.

Smell

The alluringly generous bouquet's floral register is accented with a touch of gingerbread, a La Gloria Cubana hallmark.

Taste

Spicy, honeyed flavor builds body in the second third to deliver a rich, concentrated finale. Careful maturation lends unexpected smoothness and roundness, played out in a slow, round, woodsy rhythm that never dulls.

Enjoyment

The Médaille d'Or No. 1 doesn't have the following it deserves. But it does number some ardent admirers, especially among vintage lovers who revel in the discovery of its new aromatic horizons. With its sometimes energetic last third, this cigar is for experienced palates only. The combustion is highly satisfactory for this format.

91

OVERALL RATING

Strength: 6 ½ – Uniformity: 9 – Character: 8 ½

LA GLORIA CUBANA
MÉDAILLE D'OR No. 3

Length: 6 ⅞ in. (175 mm)
Ring Gauge: 28 (11.11 mm)
Body: round
Presentation: semi-varnished box of 25

Look

With their 1970s silhouette that makes them a darling of this format's connoisseurs, these three rows of long, finely crafted chopsticks are elegance itself.

Touch

This soft cigar eschews firmness and rigidity. Its round form slides easily between the fingers and feels natural in the hand.

Smell

The floral bouquet is fresh, unctuous, and unassuming.

Taste

This understated panetela is one of the format's most aromatic, yielding pleasing spice and honeyed flavor. The regular draw is an added attraction. The light, almost distant first third builds to a rich woodsy taste in the middle third. Beware of overheating towards the end.

Enjoyment

While true to the finest La Gloria Cubana tradition, the Médaille d'Or No. 3 is atypical for its format. Its easy combustion makes it perfect for a coffee break or a reflective moment. This cigar never over-saturates but is a bit heavy and bold for beginners.

OVERALL RATING

Strength: 5 ½ – Uniformity: 7 – Character: 6 ½

• *In the same family, the **El Rey del Mundo Elegantes** is popular among lovers of lightly flavored gran panetelas.*

92

RAFAEL GONZÁLEZ SLENDERELLAS

Length: 6 ⅞ in. (175 mm)
Ring Gauge: 28 (11.11 mm)
Body: round
Presentation: traditional box of 25

Look

With its chocolate cigarette looks, this fine, round, and slender cigar seems to go on forever. It is clad in a color range running from the palest *clarisimo* to dark, warm *colorado*.

Touch

Packed sometimes to the point of rigidity, the cigar is generally both firm and supple. Depending on the tobacco, the texture runs from silky to slightly grainy.

Smell

A vegetal, subtly camphor scent pervades the body, while the foot is mild and dry. The overall impression is fresh and lively.

Taste

Exceptional combustion serves up a range of delicate woodsy aromas that are never harsh or spicy. This light, accessible, harmonious cigar will not tire you out.

Enjoyment

The Slenderellas cigar is a treat for a luxurious morning or a stolen moment. It is a favorite among female connoisseurs and may gain more of a following when fashion swings back to the elegant, less potent format.

OVERALL RATING
Strength: 5 – Uniformity: 8 – Character: 7

93

Lettre, *Anton Molnar.*

INDEX

Cigars whose names appear in italics, below do not have a page devoted to them in this book, but are referred to in relation to another cigar.

Acknowledgments

To Anton Molnar and Antoni Vives Fierro,
for having introduced art into the world of the cigar
To my mother, for her example
To my wife, for her patience
To my sister, for her complicity
To Sévan and Taline, of course.

Photographic Credits
All photographs by Matthieu Prier.

Translated from the French by Chet Weiner, Stacy Doris, and Fui Lee Luk
Copyediting: Christine Schultz-Touge and Kate Clark
Typesetting: Claude-Olivier Four
Proofreading: Anne Korkeakivi

Distributed in North America by Rizzoli International Publications, Inc.
Box set presentation and original design by Open Door, UK
Originally published in French as *Le Cigare* © Flammarion SA, 2001
First English-language edition © Flammarion SA, 2002
This revised and updated edition © Flammarion SA, 2009

www.editions.flammarion.com

09 10 11   3 2 1
ISBN: 9782080300966
Depôt légal: 03/2009
Printed by Tien Wah Press in Malaysia

GENÈVE

Kempinski Hotel – 19, quai du Mont-Blanc – 1201 Geneva
Tel. + 41 22 908 35 35
Fax + 41 22 908 35 30
www.gerard.ch
www.worldofgerard.com
www.privatebankofcigars.com
info@gerard.ch